Outside Heaven

To Sallie,

With my best wishes.
I hope you'll enjoy the
book.

Sue

S. C. McIntyre

August 2021

Outside Heaven

An Afghanistan Experience

S. C. McIntyre

OUTSIDE HEAVEN
AN AFGHANISTAN EXPERIENCE

iUniverse books may be ordered through booksellers or by contacting:

iUniverse
1663 Liberty Drive
Bloomington, IN 47403
www.iuniverse.com
844-349-9409

"All non-historical persons noted in this book have had their names changed to protect their privacy. All opinions are those of the author and not official opinions or positions of the U.S. Government or any American Embassy."

ISBN: 978-1-6632-2636-5 (sc)
ISBN: 978-1-6632-2637-2 (hc)
ISBN: 978-1-6632-2638-9 (e)

Library of Congress Control Number: 2021914846

Print information available on the last page.

iUniverse rev. date: 07/22/2021

To my mother, who anchored me in a hostile environment, and to my husband, who nurtured me and gave me wings. I have loved you both.

"If you reject the food, ignore the customs, fear the religion, and avoid the people, you might better stay home."

James Michener

Contents

Acknowledgments

A special thanks goes to so many who supported me in this effort to record my thoughts and experiences in Afghanistan when the war was new and we were newly there. For my friends who have faithfully and gently encouraged me to continue writing, even when I was easily distracted, especially my Sistas group—Janee Crotts, Marty Johnson, and Cheri Lacock. To my Tuesday morning WriteTogether Group for getting me "unstuck" and cheering me on through the tedious process of writing and rewriting this book, thank you! To my editors, who painstakingly read and reread my manuscript and did what they could to improve it. Any remaining flaws are my own. And with special appreciation for Al Lacock, who even while gravely sick gave my book its first reader's overview, thank you my dear friend. You caught many of those little editing things that can so annoy readers. And to my family: my children, Eric, Jason, and Rachel for being patient with a mother who needed to roam for so many years but always loved and cherished you. To my grandchildren, Lexie, Kate, Mitchell, and Clare—this manuscript is for you to know who your grandmother was and get a peek at what I did. And to Mike, my light, my life, my love—thank you from the bottom of my heart for being patient with me and for always being faithful to me in my need to travel far and wide. You have kept me grounded. You have kept me sane. You have made me happy. I love you.

Acronyms

ASO – Afghan Support Office

DART – Disaster Assistance Response Team, the initial US government humanitarian team that enters a disaster zone

NGO – nongovernment organization

OFDA – Office of US Foreign Disaster Assistance

UN – United Nations

UNHAS – United Nations Humanitarian Air Service

UNMAG – United Nations Mine Action Group

USAID – United States Agency for International Development

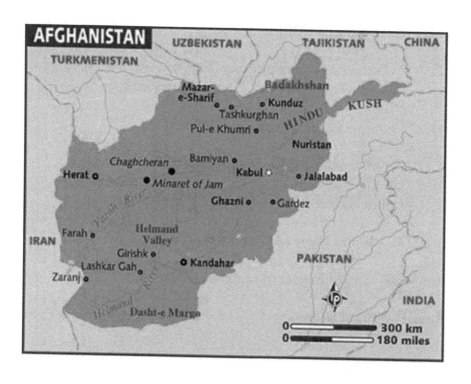

Prologue

Marietta, Georgia; Seattle, Washington; and Washington, DC

Dobbins Air Reserve Base, Marietta, Georgia — I was hiding again. I was at a special training course for US government civilian response to a chemical, biological, radiological, nuclear, and explosive (CBRNE) attack for my assignment in Afghanistan during the year of 2002. I had chosen to hide, curled into a fetal position under a tank and, during the training, started thinking about when I was a kid. Then, like now, hiding was my survival skill. Ironically, I found myself training for a job in which hiding was a skill I might need. At this particular time, the hiding was practice for incoming missiles that were expected to be a part of my days on my new assignment in Afghanistan. As I laid there, I was thinking of how much my world had shattered. My safety was always "in the world," away from home and father. And now, I'd learned, not only was my home not safe, the world was not safe. This was a major loss for me. I'd always counted on finding safety when I left my house. No one threatened me or screamed at me or cursed at me when I was away from home. How was I to deal with this new knowledge and frightening revelation?

When I was little, I always knew that to survive, I had to be invisible. When there was chaos at my house, my immediate reaction was to run and hide. If I hung around, I knew that it was only a matter of time before my father, on seeing me, would start cursing at me. He would scream, "God dammit, don't you sit around looking at me like that! If I start hitting you, I won't stop until I kill you!" I was little, five or six years old, when I first remember hearing this, and while I didn't understand it, I knew that he meant it. I didn't know why he said it, but why seemed unimportant at the time. It didn't matter whether I had done anything to cause his anger;

he just seemed to end every rant focused on me. I was one of four children and the only one who my father seemed to hate. The sun rose and set over my two brothers, and my one sister who was deaf. This disability seemed to engender in him a soft spot hidden from the rest of us. I was the lone healthy, smart girl. I seemed to irritate him just by my very existence. I used to pretend that I was not really his daughter well before I understood what that would have meant for my mother. But in reality, there was no denying I was his; my older brother and I looked like twins. My father would shout at my mother and occasionally push her down. I don't remember him ever striking her, but that was not something I stuck around to see. Like a coward, and the frightened little girl that I was, I would run and hide. That instinct was well developed in me.

I was shocked to find myself in the same position now as I trained to go into a war zone. On an intellectual level I knew the whole world was not safe, even if I had emotionally embraced this image of the world. I needed there to be someplace where I could be safe. On the whole, my gut feeling was of being safer outside my house than inside. Therefore, my senses and my psyche were shaken by witnessing the massive number of events of inhumanity in the world. After working in international humanitarian work in country after country, with all kinds of people, and witnessing humans' inhumanity toward others, I was feeling adrift. I had no firm footing in my emotional life. And this is where I was emotionally when the attacks occurred on 9/11.

I had been working successfully in international relief work for ten years, but on September 11, 2001, I was in the middle of a personal crisis. I was trying to deal with the horrors that I had seen over the past decade in war zone after war zone in Africa, in the Caucasus region of the former Soviet Union, and in the Balkan wars. The sum of my international work was wrapped up in one story after another of ordinary people who suffered unspeakable trauma at the hands of ruthless men. By the summer of 2001, I had decided that I could no longer deal with the ongoing ugliness. I needed a break.

I made the decision to stay in the United States and work in support of international relief from a headquarters position. I got a new job as the worldwide Emergency Response and Disaster Manager for World Vision, a large nongovernmental organization (NGO), in August of 2001.

I had, of course, no idea that the impending crisis of 9/11 would turn me around and take hold of my life. My planned sabbatical inside the United States, safely distanced from the tragedies of the world, was about to come crashing down around me. My escape from trauma followed me home and, literally and figuratively, landed on my doorstep.

My husband and I were living in the Crystal City neighborhood in Arlington, Virginia, just a couple of blocks from the Pentagon when it was hit. The burning building could be seen directly from our eleventh-floor balcony. The smoke permeated our apartment, and use of the balcony was not possible for many weeks. But much more important by far was that my second son, Jason, was in one of the World Trade Center towers the morning of the 9/11 attack in New York City.

Jason was on the eighty-ninth floor of the South Tower. His office wasn't there, but he had gone to the towers that morning for a meeting planned to start at 9:00 a.m. As he checked in to the building, as was required, with ID and photo, his name was pulled up on a roster saved from previous visits. He was impressed and expressed his admiration for the security system, saying to the guard, "Boy, you guys are really on top of things here."

"Yeah, we check everyone entering," the guard proudly replied. "After the attack in 1993, we tightened up ground control. No one wanders in." How quickly those words would be rendered meaningless when planes attacked from the sky within a matter of minutes.

Once Jason was cleared through security, he went up the elevators to his meeting. He had just arrived in the office and was standing at a window overlooking the courtyard, and the North Tower, making a phone call prior to the start of his meeting. That meeting never happened. The first plane slammed into the North Tower at 8:46 a.m. My son watched in stunned amazement as the American Airlines jet flew straight into the massive structure directly in front of him. It was almost exactly at eye level, and he could see the pilot's and passengers' faces through the plane's windows. He later described it as watching a horror movie unfold in slow motion. When the plane hit the building, there was complete silence—a testament to the soundproofing in each tower. His colleagues at the conference table, with their backs to the windows, heard nothing. Their only awareness was of a slight shaking, and they thought that an earthquake had occurred. Jason turned and exclaimed, "Holy shit! A plane just flew into the North Tower!" Apparently, others' first thought was that he meant a small, privately piloted plane had hit the tower. They immediately saw that this was not the case, as evidenced by the explosion of flames. Jason said, "We have to get out of here."

Several of the older men, all of whom had offices in the building, responded, "No, just sit down, and we'll wait for emergency instructions. That's the protocol."

Jason grabbed his briefcase and said, "No, I'm out of here. I'm not staying in a neighborhood where planes are flying into buildings." He was unaware of how prophetic his words were to become.

Seventeen minutes later, at 9:03 a.m., the second plane hit the South Tower at the fifty-first-floor level. I have lived those seventeen minutes over and over in my mind. I equate that length of time to the time that many of my daily activities of life require. I timed myself during a fire drill in my office building, where I had to exit from the eighth floor—only the eighth floor. It took longer than seventeen minutes to get out. I could be standing in line for a cup of coffee at a coffee shop. It often took close to seventeen minutes to get my cup of coffee and get on my way. I carried my laundry down the stairs to the washers and dryers in the basement from my eleventh floor apartment. Again, the seventeen-minute limit was approached. And then I think of my son during his time of exiting the towers and those critical first thirty-nine flights that had to be descended to get below the impact of the second plane on the fifty-first floor. My breath always catches as I think of him racing against time. I remember each encounter on that fateful decent as he recounted for me. He took time to speak to his colleagues at the meeting, resulting in a brief discussion of the merits of waiting for emergency instructions or not. Then Jason ran through the hallways telling others who were out of sight of windows about the attack. He was encouraging people to leave immediately. When he got to the bank of elevators, a crowd was already forming, so he and two other brave, young men began shepherding the younger, healthier people toward the stairs and assisting the less strong, older ones onto the elevators. When the elevators were full, they knew it would take some time before they came back up to get them. And so they too began to run down the stairs from eighty-nine floors up. It is miraculous that he made it below the fifty-first floor level before the second plane hit. I think of my handsome son, who in my mind's eye becomes my adorable three-year-old, caught up in a crisis beyond imagining. What mother would not instantly think of her child as the little one she had sheltered and cared for? But on 9/11, he was well out of my reach at that "life-or-death" moment. I was remembering and reliving those moments of impotency that later drove me to go to Afghanistan. It was my way of doing something in response to that trauma on that awful day.

During the actual attacks on 9/11, I was in Seattle, starting a new job with World Vision. I was staying at a hotel and woke early to go to an all-night megastore. I needed to buy something to wear to the office. As fate would have it, my luggage had been lost on my flight the day before, and I didn't have anything fresh or professional to wear to the office. I didn't feel comfortable presenting myself on my first day of work in my travel jeans, so I left my hotel room about 5:30 a.m. Pacific Time, exactly twenty-six minutes prior to the first attack that would occur three thousand miles away in New York City. It took me about one hour to shop and get back to my hotel. Once I was back in my room and as I was getting ready for work, I turned on the television to see the news of the day—and there were the attacks. I watched in stunned disbelief as I saw a plane crash into the North Tower and burst into flames. Within seconds, the news footage shifted and showed the second plane crash into the South Tower. I froze in front of the television. How could this be happening? My first thoughts were of my son, who worked nearby on Wall Street. I called his office immediately only to get the news that he had gone to a meeting that morning in the World Trade Center. Agony! I was stunned. I turned to look again at the TV screen repeatedly showing the planes crashing into the towers. As new footage was collected, I saw it all from different angles. I was alone in my hotel room and frightened. My stomach went into knots, and I immediately felt nauseated. I remember turning around in circles trying to decide what I should do, what I *could* do. It was shortly after six thirty that morning—nine thirty in New York—when I collapsed on the side of the bed and cried. I sat paralyzed for some minutes, assimilating the fact that my son was somewhere in the towers. In my panic and confusion, I could only look at the television. My dread grew as I feared that I had lost my son forever. My first thoughts were to call him. I tried but there was no getting through the crammed telephone lines into New York City. I tried to call my other children and my husband in Washington, DC, and then saw the attack on the Pentagon. Now my panic knew no bounds. My entire family was on the East Coast, two of them right in the line of attack. I was frantic about my family's safety. I continued trying to get in touch with them to no avail.

I decided to go into the World Vision office, where I could be with others. It seemed a better option than staying in the hotel alone. I knew I wouldn't be worth much once in the office, but it passed the time and people were kind to me. As the hours passed, I realized there would be no easy way to get home. Nothing had prepared me for how I felt being isolated from everyone I knew and loved as I watched the towers burst into flames and collapse into rubble. It was four interminable hours before I heard from Jason. He finally got a call out to me. I'll never forget hearing his voice after fearing he had been caught and killed in the towers. I listened to him tell me that he was unhurt, had made it out, and would tell me more when he saw me. After that, I immediately began working on a plan to get home. It took me seven days to organize a realistic way to travel. In that time, Jason had driven down to our apartment in Crystal City. He was in shock and needed to be close to family, and Mike was there for him. I later learned that he was the only one to make it out alive from the group in his meeting. Those very people who tried to convince Jason to wait for emergency instructions had perished.

This is not a story of about Jason's path to healing and reentry to his normal life but of my response and resulting experiences as I made the decision to put my professional skills to use in some manner. I didn't immediately know how or what form that would take but felt pulled to respond. Though my many years of work in war-torn countries had taken a toll on me, my first response was to go back in the field. Given the initial news from Washington and the government, I knew that there would be some military response. And having been in other countries in crisis, I understood the suffering that was to come to the innocent people in Afghanistan if there was an attack on their soil as was being discussed. The United States seemed committed to retaliating for these horrific attacks. The news reports were full of Osama bin Laden, Al Qaeda, soldiers and their safe havens in Afghanistan. The Taliban, as the governing body in

Afghanistan at the time, refused to allow America access to the terrorist. I knew if they didn't, it would mean war with Afghanistan. I had seen how war, any war, was most traumatic on innocent civilians, who always suffered behind the scenes.

My specialty was working in such war zones. If I was to go, as I felt I needed to do, I would have to convince my husband and family. My husband was, of course, worried about me going into another war zone, and I wondered if my son might need me at home. I decided to talk to him about this as soon as I could. I didn't know how he would handle the long-term trauma resulting from being in the attack. My mind was reeling as I was stuck in Seattle trying to arrange my travel back east.

First things first, though, I had to make my way back home from Seattle. Almost one week passed before planes began flying again. I got on a flight as soon as possible. I had tried all means of travel—trains, buses, rental cars, everything short of hitchhiking—to try to get home, but nothing was available. I therefore found myself flying again within a week of the attacks.

Being in an airplane suddenly became very stressful. Everyone was anxious, and the scene at the Seattle airport was chaotic. There were new rules, new lines, and short tempers from the accumulated fear that we all carried within ourselves. People were confused as to what they needed to do. Suddenly everyone's bags were being searched, meaning more delays. There were new X-ray scanners, and the poor, overstressed security workers were trying to execute new procedures in the midst of the confusion. Eventually, we boarded.

"Please introduce yourselves to the passengers on your right and left," said the pilot. "Get to know each other, and we'll all feel better. I know this is a tense time and many of you are scared. My colleagues and I will be doing our best to make this a comfortable and safe trip back to Washington." The voice was soothing. He told us that he was locked in his cabin and would fly us safely home. It was a new beginning in airport travel.

And so it began, my first flight after 9/11. I was so anxious to get home and be with my family. My husband had been telling me that Jason was doing okay but was very nervous. Unfortunately, neither of them could get away from the daily reminder of the attacks with the smoking Pentagon outside our apartment windows.

I finally arrived home. My priority was, of course, to take my son in my arms. Later we talked about the attacks, life plans, and the road ahead. Jason was shaken and unsure if he could go back into the city, ride in the confined subways, be in tall buildings, or fly. All of these things were necessary for his daily life and work. Mike and I were loath to push him, and we assured him our home was open to him as long as he needed. But I knew him. He is a fighter and a survivor. Sure enough, within a week he felt he needed to get back to the city and confront his fears.

"I'm not sure how I'll do my job, Mom, or how I'll manage my life in the city," he admitted one night while we were standing on the balcony.

"I'm not sure what to tell you," I said. "All I know is that we cannot let the terrorists win. And if you let them destroy your life, they will have won. You got out. You survived. Now you need to figure out how to go on. I'm thinking of going to work in Afghanistan. You know I can't go back if the terrorists win, right?"

"Right. But I'm surprised you're thinking of going out again," he said with a good degree of concern. "I know you're tired and had decided to stay home for a while. Overall, I'm not sure if it's a good idea for you to go to Afghanistan."

"I know. Your father is also concerned," I replied. "I spoke with him about it, but I feel like it would be a way for me to react in a positive manner. I can manage programs there to assist the civilians who will suffer terribly for crimes they did not commit and were completely out of their control. I think it will be tangible proof that America is stronger than these evil men. What do you say I go there and you go to New York?"

Jason was thoughtful for a while. Finally, he said, "Deal. I go and you go. Let's see what we can do."

It was a way for both of us to start again.

As I went back to work in our Washington office, I was terribly shaken but continued to feel the tug to do more than I was. I was sad, angry, tired, and discouraged. I didn't know how I would get to Afghanistan; I just knew I had to. This decision was closely tied to surviving and seemed a reasonable and responsive way to carry on after tragedy.

I continued working for World Vision, where I had the opportunity to begin designing a response for Afghanistan in the immediate months after the attacks. I was happy to be doing this, but it weighed on me that I was not there in the country to work. I decided to either convince World Vision to send me to Afghanistan to work on the programs we were busy establishing or find another way to go. My chance came when I got a call in January from the Office of U.S. Foreign Disaster Assistance (OFDA). They offered me the job of leading the US government's humanitarian team in Afghanistan. I jumped at the offer even while knowing I was still processing both the tower attacks and my previous burnout. I wondered how I would react to the kinds of extreme suffering that I knew I would find there.

And so, just four months after the 9/11 attacks, I was heading to Afghanistan. I was already well prepared for the academics and fundamentals of my job but emotionally fragile. I started my journey in the last week in January 2002. My head was full of family, the Washington briefings I had received, and my new assignment.

There was no question in my mind that this job was meant for me, my next journey.

Chapter 1

My Beginning in International Work, 1991

I didn't start my professional life as a diplomat. I was a late-in-life bloomer to this work of international disaster relief. It was a second career for me, and I needed to learn a lot while carrying forward all of my other life skills. I was a licensed physical therapist and had worked for many years in the United States in various hospitals and rehabilitation settings. I really enjoyed my work but felt drawn to expand my life experiences. I had always wanted to travel and live among foreign cultures and peoples. I was not sure how I would accomplish that goal until, one day, I saw an advertisement that caught my eye. It was an ad in the *American Physical Therapy Journal* seeking therapists to work in Armenia following a massive earthquake that had left many thousands of people injured and handicapped. They were looking for professionals to provide direct PT treatments and set up a curriculum to train Armenian PTs, as well as someone to be a PT department director and set up and run the newly developed Red Cross rehabilitation center in the capital city of Yerevan, Armenia. It sounded like a perfect fit for me, so I applied for the director's position and got the job. Luckily for me, my husband, Mike, a hospital administrator, was on board with this adventure, and he found a job managing a newly constructed plastic and reconstructive surgery hospital unit. This was in conjunction with another internationally supported response for the earthquake victims. Both of us were bringing forward our existing professional skills into this new area of work in the early 1990s. Our children were in various stages of finishing their college studies, so our home responsibilities were such that we could pick up and go. I knew the kids were surprised by our decision. It was planned to be a one-year adventure but, of course, changed as we began our work overseas. We both loved living and working abroad.

I began my international work with the American Red Cross, International Division doing physical therapy in Armenia. I felt drawn to the work and really thought I had found the job I wanted to do. From that beginning, I worked hard to learn about international relief. I gradually branched off to work on other programs, and in other countries, for several different NGOs.

Immediately after my two and a half years in Armenia with the American Red Cross, I went to work for the United Methodist Committee on Relief (UMCOR). I stayed with them for a total of five years. I worked in Liberia, which was suffering terribly from a protracted civil war that had torn the country apart and caused untold suffering for its people. I stayed in that country for almost a year coping with the rebel fighters and the chaotic government. This was my first experience in a war zone. I learned about the security risks and worked closely with the United Nations (UN) and other NGOs to provide assistance. It was a real baptism by fire for me in the chaos and dangers of war. In this country I was dealing with unregulated militias and ongoing abuse of civilians, including rape of the women and girls. It was a dangerous situation and, at the time, I was not working for the US government; as such, I did not have the level of protection afforded me within an embassy with its resources. It was a hard assignment, and I was on edge much of the time but most especially when in the jungle and remote villages. In spite of this, we were able to do some good work for the civilians.

Following Liberia, I went to Haiti to assist UMCOR with setting up an office and bringing in aid for the Haitian people following Jean-Bertrand Aristide's abrupt and disruptive departure. My year there added to my knowledge of working in undeveloped and unstable countries. Afterward, I went to Bosnia and stayed there for three years developing programs and leading a large office that served the Bosnians as they struggled to survive and then recover from the years of war during the breakup of Yugoslavia. This was a war zone with multiple sides and complicated issues being disputed. The people were caught up in these disputes being settled by guns, land mines, and bombs. Bosnia spilled over into Kosovo, where I changed the focus of my work. I started working for the US government for the first time there. I shifted from providing direct services for the people in need to funding those programs on behalf of the US government. It was during my work in Kosovo that I met my future boss for my Afghanistan assignment.

By the time I went to Afghanistan, I had a total of ten years of NGO work and a couple years of US government work under my belt. The official name of my office was the US Agency for International Development, Office of US Foreign Disaster Assistance. Its mission statement is threefold: 1) save human lives, 2) reduce human suffering, and 3) reduce the economic and social loss due to disaster. What great goals! It was the best place in the US government for me to work. I loved my job.

I was a fifty-year-old grandmother by the time I headed to Afghanistan. Many times I asked myself, *Are you sure you should be doing this?* What other grandmother would be jumping on Humvees, wearing *shalwar kameez*, arguing with officers in the US military, and living underground in a bunker? I think my children might have liked me to be the sweet-little-old-lady kind of grandmother who knitted, baked chocolate chip cookies, and stayed home to babysit grandbabies. Instead, I was running off to foreign lands at war.

Chapter 2

Internal Struggles

Islamabad, Pakistan, January 2002

In the midst of traveling to start my Afghanistan assignment, meeting my team, and beginning this new job, I continued to struggle with my inner demons. Personal demons have a way of chasing you everywhere, even into Afghanistan.

I was already stressed to the breaking point when I returned home from Bosnia and Kosovo in the summer of 2001, struggling to come to terms with all I had seen, heard, and experienced over the past decade. I was in counseling to learn how to cope with the craziness and cruelty that I saw during many months of work in hostile locations. Prior to working for the US government as a part of their diplomat corps overseas, my international work had brought me in direct contact with recipients of the humanitarian programs. Those early years brought their own kind of trauma. I had been attacked in Armenia, where a man broke into my apartment and stabbed my roommate. I survived but suffered terrible posttraumatic stress. I worked hard and felt that I had dealt with that first threatening incident. In addition to this event were the assignments in places at war where I was lost in the jungle and attacked in both Liberia and in Cote d'Ivoire in street violence. I had reached a real crisis in my faith. It was a mystery to me how the God that I believed in could let these horrible things happen, not so much to me but to the people I was trying to serve. I always knew I had an out. I could go home, but not so for most of the people I was meeting. It felt bigger than just the "Why Bad Things Happen to Good People" question posed in Rabbi Harold S. Kushner's book. People inflicted damage on one another in ways that were beyond my imagination. How did a sniper on a hillside outside of Sarajevo shoot an elderly woman hobbling to a public water fountain to fetch water for her family? How did a man shoot children on a playground in Kosovo? How did a man kill a pregnant woman, extract the baby, kill it, and then replace it in her womb with a bomb rigged to explode when she was examined? How did men in the UN peacekeepers forcefully rape desperate women in exchange for food in Liberia? The inhumanity was everywhere, in every religious group. All of it was so confusing. When I asked for answers, I was told that the old woman was a disembodied figure seen through the rifle scope of a sniper. The children slaughtered on the playground were the children of men who had slaughtered the shooter's family and left their gouged-out eyeballs on the kitchen table for him to find when he returned home. The raped women were freely exchanging sex for food. The stories were personal to me as I had often looked into the eyes of the victims. I found it hard to internalize. I wasn't even sure if I should internalize those ugly things.

I needed to attend to my mental health as well as my physical health during every assignment. But this time, heading into Afghanistan, it was different. I was coming off of the 9/11 attacks. My plans had changed with our family's very personal experience of that event. My original idea to take some time away from direct fieldwork fell by the wayside.

When I left the United States, I was feeling vulnerable. I was disconnecting from family, most especially from my husband Mike, who usually shared my overseas work most closely. He was ambivalent about my taking this assignment and worried about my safety. We had grown apart with the strain of previous assignments, often separated for months at a time. It was not easy to sort out daily issues, never mind big issues, when one partner was halfway around the world from the other.

I was having a hard time identifying the cause of my disassociation from loved ones. I didn't feel that they understood the scope of my work or the daily demands I faced when in the field. I was caught between being overly descriptive and worrying them or being vague about the dangers, pressures, and complexities, which meant they could not understand how many things I was dealing with. Maybe it was just that I was feeling so burned out and tired of the hostilities and cruelties in the world. Whatever it was, it was eating at me. I looked at the others in the diplomatic corps and wondered if any of them were having or had experienced these job-related stresses. As it turned out, my feelings were more common than I realized. All of this was going on during the early 2000s, well before USAID and the State Department began offering routine psychological support for persons separated from families and in high-stress locations, such as Afghanistan, Sudan, and Iraq.

As usual, the beginning of every assignment was hectic. I worked twelve- to fourteen-hour days, often without time off on weekends. The schedule kept me from looking too closely at myself. I managed in this denial process for a while as my team and I struggled with making arrangements to travel to Pakistan. And then there were the details of traveling safely in and out of the evolving war in Afghanistan. I was caught up in the ongoing myriad details of finding accommodations in order to go into Kabul. There were no hotels or bed-and-breakfasts to rent at that time. I was constructing and reporting all our activities every day for Washington. We were working in Islamabad, Pakistan, from a rented office space for the first few weeks, which added a layer of complexity to reaching the Afghan people. We had to take short, quick trips into Kabul. Every trip into Afghanistan had to be approved by Washington; supported by the UN flights, the only means of foreigners entering Afghanistan; and then supported by our international NGO partners already located in Kabul for accommodations in their guesthouses. I had to confirm bed availability for each trip. Because we had no logistics support set up in Kabul, we also needed to borrow drivers and cars when there. Traveling into a war is dangerous, as expected, but what the general public often does not understand is the hours of logistics planning needed prior to any trip. Each trip demanded tight coordination with an NGO; approval from the American embassy in Islamabad, which had control of all US government diplomatic activities in Afghanistan through its Afghan Support Office (ASO); and final blessing from Washington, which was eleven hours behind us. Every trip had to be planned to the last detail days in advance, but last-minute changes in response to the situation on the ground were inevitable. Because of all this, I was anxious to establish our team in Kabul and set up our own support system—drivers, translators, cooks, and most importantly, safe housing. These concerns pulled me in multiple directions every day. Thank goodness my great team was managing the actual program planning that addressed the direct needs of millions of people suffering in Afghanistan.

We all went about our days, busy with various job responsibilities. My number-one concern was the safety of any team member who traveled into Afghanistan for work. Our initial forays into Kabul were limited to two to three days at a time to reduce risks. We then returned to Islamabad for a week or more of additional logistics planning and paperwork. Flying in and out, albeit on UN flights, was always a risk. When in Kabul, we initially stayed in downtown locations, outside of the American embassy, which increased the risks, especially for women. I knew that I would be much less stressed once we got permission from Washington and the American embassy in Kabul to establish ourselves in our own safe housing or inside the embassy with the safety that provided. The challenge in the embassy was finding bed space. At that time America was still using the old embassy, which had very limited office space, had no living accommodations, and was filled with US Marines. The issue was finally resolved after a lot of negotiation, and our team was given five spaces inside the American embassy compound. This meant that I had to cut my team back by three people. Gender was a consideration because our assigned spaces consisted of three for males in the male-only area of the embassy and two for women in the female group room. My team ended up consisting of two women—a food specialist and me. The three men were a program officer, an information officer, and a safety and security officer. They were a great group of highly skilled teammates, and for this I was always grateful. They made my job easier, and because of their professionalism, they needed very little direct supervision. All of this provided a strong support system for me.

I wanted to do a good job for the people of Afghanistan, for my team, and for myself. But I still needed to attend to my personal feelings—a tall order, I realize as I look back on it over the distance of many years. It's a common belief that those working overseas fall into three broad categories: those running away from something, those running toward something, and those wanting to do some good in the world. The last is by far the smallest group. While I think that doing good deeds is a motivating factor, it is often nudged into action by either of the first two considerations. I was a combination, as are most people. I wanted to do some good in the world, but I was also running away. I didn't want to deal with my own insecurities or confusion at home. I was burned out, and I hadn't stayed off the treadmill of humanitarian assistance long enough to face myself squarely and work on my family issues prior to having Afghanistan thrust upon me.

Obviously, feeling disconnected from my family was not helped by my being physically separated from them and all that was familiar. I wanted to make my life work. I wanted to be home and happy with my husband and family, who were so supportive of me, and I wanted to feel free and fulfilled in my professional life. I wanted it all.

Chapter 3

Getting to Kabul

Any trip to Afghanistan is long. For me, it began in Washington, DC near the end of January 2002. The planning was taking place on two fronts: first in the Ronald Reagan Building that houses USAID and second at home with family and friends. My professional responsibilities included getting my diplomatic passport updated, completing my top-secret security clearance procedures, and being briefed on the scope of my job. My time in Washington was limited as those in charge were anxious to get me out in the field and pick up the leadership for team members already posted in Pakistan. The team had begun the initial work on assessments, program planning, and funding needs for Afghanistan. The American embassy in Islamabad carried the weight of all support for the staff in and out of Afghanistan through their Afghan Support Office (ASO). This was necessary because, at that time, there was not a fully functioning American embassy in Kabul. The ASO would remain active for a number of years, even after the Kabul embassy opened, because the Kabul location was limited in staff, space, and services.

My personal and family preparations included a long list of issues consisting of discussing my assignment as best I could with family members to reassure them that I would be okay. I felt a need to convince them of why I *needed* to go, to provide them as much information as I could, or was allowed to; to complete any last-minute trainings that were required; to get my medical clearance and all shots required; and to decide what to pack given the cultural considerations of appropriate dress for women. Since I was not military, I had no uniform, of course. I usually planned on being prepared for a wide range of dress needs at embassies. These included apparel for field trips in harsh conditions in rural areas, daily office wear, and any formal embassy events. My normal assignments allowed for buying local wear as needed, but I was unsure of what would be available in Kabul. I usually wore comfortable, American-style business clothes within the embassy. I wasn't sure that the buying local option would be available in Kabul as no American diplomats had lived there for longer than a dozen years, so advice was limited.

I discussed the assignment thoroughly with my husband. My leaving would impact him the most since, at this stage, the kids were all living and working outside of the house and in different states. Mike was a real trooper, and as always his support of me and my career was critical. My safety was of great concern. Neither of us knew how this war in Afghanistan would unfold. We were in the very early days of the conflict, so there was still very little US military presence in the country and sparse staffing at the embassy. We had read that the United States had Special Forces and some CIA agents in the country fighting with the Afghanistan Northern Alliance. The Taliban had control of Kabul and most of the country at the time. I had not been deployed into quite such an unknown environment before, so the normal tension and concerns were amplified. There were many long hours of discussing the "what ifs", some of which were routine but many that were quite new. I was not usually advised to get my will in order, leave instructions concerning my remains, and talk about these hard issues with family and friends before leaving. I didn't want to burden my kids with these difficult subjects, and since they were not at home or involved in the day-to-day preparations, it was easy to avoid. But Mike and I talked in great detail about all the possibilities. He respected my years of preparation and my personal skills, knew of my training, and trusted in my intelligence, but he feared the unknown for me. I was able to reassure him of only so much. The truth was that I did not know what it would be like on the ground. Our office had never had staff stationed inside Afghanistan before so there was very little information available on the current situation. What little reliable information I could get came from our NGO partners who were operating in Afghanistan and were being supported by our funds. These organizations included Save the Children, CARE, Mercy Corps, and World Vision, to mention just a few. They all had US offices in Washington, and I was able to discuss existing and planned programs with them, including staff conditions inside Afghanistan prior to leaving. Some of these discussions offered information on the actual living conditions and safety precautions that staff took to survive in Afghanistan. Every bit of knowledge brought both reassurance and worry to my family and me. Generally, I made decisions as best I could, knowing everyone starting up the American embassy would be in the same boat. There were a lot of unknowns in planning this assignment for all of us. In the end, Mike and I agreed that I would go to Afghanistan for a six-month initial period and then re-evaluate. The kids, to some degree, were used to me doing these overseas assignments and so accepted it with grace and patience. Their knowledge and understanding of the privations and danger were limited by the very foreignness of my work. I think they pictured me in a secure American embassy. I did not disabuse them of this vision.

I proceeded with all my personal plans—got my will updated, medical tests done, shots endured, and modest clothes packed for cold winters and hot summers, as was common in Afghanistan. I had no idea of what laundry facilities would be available but packed as best I could. The outerwear I chose was dark and practical in nature. Unfortunately, outerwear for winter can be bulky. I went with a limited but good, warm winter coat, boots, and accessories. Summer wear, being less bulky, was easier. My shoes were simple pairs of flats, flip-flops, and sneakers for leisure wear and field trips. I needed to get all my clothes and hygiene products for six months in two suitcases.

The initial leg of the trip took me from Washington, DC to Islamabad, Pakistan, where I stayed in a local guesthouse while working with my team of eight colleagues. The Islamabad team consisted of three program officers, one food officer, one refugee specialist, one communications officer, one safety and security officer, and one administrative officer. We ranged in age from twenty-six years old to sixty-seven years old with experience levels from one year out of graduate school to thirty years of security experience. It is always a wonder how teams formed and bonded quickly when put in dangerous situations. I counted on their professionalism kicking in and was not disappointed with this team. Among the various skill sets were also various personalities that added interest and charm. On my team was a

13

quiet, shy one, Laura, my food specialist; a comic, Jeff, my program officer; the gruff, tough one, Larry, my security specialist who was the oldest of the team members; a diligent one, Danny, my information officer; and a prankster, Amal, my administrator and logistics officer. I loved them all by the end of our time together.

We knew we would have to live in Islamabad until the permanent housing arrangements in Kabul could be made, so we took frequent, short trips into Kabul to evaluate the situation and make on-the-ground, informed decisions. There were questions of where to live; what was available to rent; and who to hire locally for administrative staff, housing staff, translators, and drivers to be answered before we could present a permanent, in country plan acceptable to Washington. Critical questions as to our safety also had to be sorted out. All these issues had to be resolved before we could concentrate solely on our primary role, that of assisting the vulnerable Afghan civilians during the early days of war.

When living in Islamabad, we had to buy our airline tickets to go to Kabul through the UN Humanitarian Air Services (UNHAS) office, which had been established for the specific purpose of providing a safe option for humanitarian travel in crisis zones and now worked to get us into Afghanistan. In February 2002, UNHAS provided the only air transportation available for civilians to fly in and out of Kabul. They offered two flights per week. Our office supported this operation financially and, as such, was given some priority in getting tickets. With the onset of the war, all other commercial airlines had canceled their services. The entire process of obtaining a ticket, checking in, and boarding the plane was unique to flying on a UN carrier.

I called their local office, inquired about days and times of flights, and had my name put on the roster. I was instructed to appear two hours early on the day of the flight to check in at the UN ticket office, which was located in a house in one of the residential districts of Islamabad. UN workers composed the airline staff, who would handle the reservations for each flight, secure and clear the required documents needed for each passenger, receive payments from either individuals or organizations responsible for them, and then email notifications of the exact time and place to their offices. Once I checked in, I had to wait for the final call to board a bus that drove the passengers to a nearby airport. I traveled alone from my office on my initial trip into Kabul because I could only find sleeping arrangements for one. Some of the team had returned the week before, so they stayed back for this trip.

The plane I was a small twelve-seater with limited room for bags. The total cargo and passenger weight was tightly monitored. The staff weighed the bags and each passenger. To the chagrin of the few of us women on the roster, it was a public weighing on a big, flat, metal scale. It made me think of a feed-store scale and the unflattering message that conveyed. The weight of each passenger was then called out to the recorder a few feet away. I had noticed that one of the young, slim female travelers took this public weighing in stride, but thank goodness, there was another older and not-quite-so-slim woman who scrunched up her nose as her weight was called out. I wasn't alone in my horror at having my weight publicly revealed. There was a polite, no-eye-contact moment during which everyone pretended not to hear those weights called out. As my weight was announced, I cringed and pointed to my heavy backpack, which was weighed with me. *Ugh, no secrets here*, I realized, not for the first or last time. I was counting on my nod toward my backpack to indicate it was heavy. It occurred to me that vanity might be the death of me; I might have preferred to lie as they planned the flight's weight capacity and fuel needs. The one saving grace for me as an American was that the weight was given in kilograms, which was less familiar and *sounded* less heavy than pounds. At the completion of this public weighing, my check-in was completed.

One element of travel was always the same—after check-in, there was the wait. I was ready to line up for transit to the UN flight with my one bag and my "heavy" backpack. I had used the UNHAS system in many other countries, so it was familiar to me. The waiting room in Islamabad was outside on the front lawn of the office, so my most immediate desire was to find a shady spot on the ground. I sat next to a tree on the grass, still damp from rain the previous night, and braced myself, literally and figuratively, for my first trip into Afghanistan. Twelve passengers waited in the heat to be bussed to the small, local airport behind the Islamabad International Airport. We all sat on the ground. Some of the passengers obviously knew one another and talked, while the newcomers like myself covertly eyed the others as we waited.

As I looked around, the travelers were the usual suspects on a trip like this: UN workers, NGO workers, and foreign government workers. I started saying hello, doing my established airport networking routine whenever I was starting a new job. I began introducing myself and asking questions of those around me to get as much information about Kabul as possible. I wanted to know who the other passengers were and what their jobs were. I was curious as to where they would be staying while there. Every bit of information I could glean on entering a foreign country was of value to me; and Afghanistan was a big unknown. Some of the other passengers had been to Kabul before, and they quickly became the center of attention as some of us began asking them questions. I listened attentively. They were the local experts of the moment on living in Afghanistan. There, under the sun and next to a tree, I got my first local Afghanistan orientation. My briefings in Washington had been formal and given by people who had never actually been to Kabul. As such, they lacked detail on much of the most practical information I wanted, such as the process of entering the country, restrictions might I be faced with, security concerns at the airport, where the American embassy driver would wait for me, and whether there were any public facilities at the airport. In Washington, I got a lot of political briefing details, program and budget goals, staffing plans, and such, but I did not learn where I could get a drink of clean water, how to get my bags through customs, or what the living conditions in Kabul were like. For these details, I needed to talk to people who had been there. Hence the canvasing of the group sitting around me. A seasoned UN worker explained that only three restaurants in Kabul were open to foreigners and described the menus. An NGO worker who looked well-worn and very young said that I needed a man with me to talk to any Afghan official. Also critical was the information that I needed to not only cover my head when with Afghan men but also that I should have blouses with sleeves that extended below my elbows. Thankfully, that wasn't a problem as it was February and quite cold in Kabul, but still it was good to know for the future. Another bit of information was that I should not sit in the front seat with any Afghan driver or I would be presumed to be a whore. *Okay ...*

One nice-looking older lady was among the passengers waiting, and I went up to her to say hello. She had a tall elegance about her, and when

I spoke, she turned to me with a smile and warmth in her eyes. Oh, how encouraging that was to me on that stressful morning as I was anticipating this first trip into Afghanistan. To my amazement, I learned that she was to be my new boss in Afghanistan. She was the temporary Charge d'Affaires, the ranking representative at an embassy of the US government to a hosting government until a permanent ambassador could be appointed and arrived in country. As such, she was a terribly important person for me to connect with as all my future negotiations regarding bringing in my team and living in Kabul would have to be approved by her. This was really a great opportunity for me to spend some personal time with her. We talked at length about Kabul, and while this was her first trip in since 9/11, what a lovely surprise it was for me to learn that she had lived in Kabul as a young political officer at the US embassy in the 1960s. I quizzed her for information on what Kabul had been like when she was there. She smiled and began telling me of the life she had experienced there forty years earlier. I listened with amazement as she regaled me with story after story of the Afghan people and the flower-lined streets of Kabul. She was a delightful font of information. Soon a number of the other passengers scooted over closer to hear her talk. She told us about the openness of the society, of the women in Western clothes attending the university, and of the interest in culture and plays and music. She even spoke with great enthusiasm of the joint theatrical group she had been part of that included Afghans and Westerners from a number of the embassies and was very popular. They would put on plays, musicals, and dramatic presentations for anyone who wanted to come. We were all amazed at the notion of this kind of Afghanistan. As we sat mesmerized with stories of her past experiences, we momentarily forgot the reality of what it was like in Kabul today. Could there be a hope of reviving this past if the international community worked hard? It seemed like more of a possible dream than it had prior to hearing her stories. It was a new vision for me and seemed like a worthy goal. I sat there pondering my new assignment on the heels of the tragedy in New York. Did the shadow of one past reality preclude the possibility of this potential future reality?

Her storytelling ended abruptly when the UN van arrived to take us to the airport and we all jumped up to gather our belongings. Once we were loaded and ready to go, a new hush settled over all of us. As for me, I became acutely aware that I was really on my way into mysterious Afghanistan. I started thinking of this place that sent terrorists to America and yet was also once a place for families and a playground for Western diplomats assigned there. What a long trip, emotionally and physically, this had been from my hotel room in Seattle watching the towers collapse on TV, to my apartment balcony in Crystal City, Virginia, overlooking the charred remains on the side of the Pentagon, to Kabul. I was full of conflicting emotions, including gratitude, for my chance to be there. I was anxious to get there and start my work. I was less enthusiastic about tackling my personal issues that had followed me to Kabul, but I had not forgotten them.

We left the UN office and turned down the wide streets of Islamabad toward the airport and Kabul. The small airport was chaotic, as expected. The most urgent need now was to stay with my group. We proceeded through the commercial terminal and out the back door to a waiting UN plane. As we walked onto the tarmac, our plane was clearly marked with the familiar blue UN logo and parked away from the commercial Pakistani airplanes. We walked quickly, carrying all our luggage and backpacks. At the steps leading to the plane, we turned over our one allowable piece of luggage to a local UN baggage handler, who loaded them into the back of the small plane. Then I climbed on board for the first of many trips I would take into Kabul and into war.

There was a hush as we lifted off. It marked the beginning of a true adventure for all of us. Even the most experienced among us sensed that this would be a momentous journey into a country that was in the first stages of war with most of the Western world. For many of us, it was our maiden voyage into an active war zone.

This assignment was my first time working alongside the US military as it actively engaged in fighting a war. I wondered what that would be like. My job was so different from theirs. I would not be carrying a gun, wearing a helmet or bulletproof vest, or trying to capture or kill anyone. I would be bringing lifesaving humanitarian assistance to the vulnerable civilians in the country, some of whom might have male family members fighting alongside our soldiers and some fighting against our soldiers. My target population would concentrate on the women, children, and elderly, but still they might be family to Taliban. *How will this work with the US troops?* I wondered.

As usual, our UN aircraft equipment was an old, discarded plane from one of the member nations that had been retrofitted for humanitarian use. As such, the acoustics inside were much worse than the more familiar, newer commercial aircraft. Because of the high noise volume, and because most of us were feeling rather introspective, there was little conversation. I know I was deep in thought, trying to be very present in the moment. It was only a forty-five-minute flight.

As soon as we entered Afghan airspace, there was a palpable shift in the tension in the plane. We all knew there was a chance of being shot down. We were quiet, each going deeper into our own thoughts.

When I got my first peek out the window at the snow-covered mountains and crusty, barren land, I knew that my life was about to change. I sent up a silent prayer that I would be safe, do a good job, and serve my country well on this assignment. I had no training in American warfare and very little in survival on this, my maiden voyage into this war zone. I had not been issued any personal protective equipment and hadn't even thought to ask for any. The more usual move for embassy personnel would be exit a country when the US military was entering to actively engage in combat. But here I was, charging into the unknown with my fellow UN, humanitarian, and embassy workers.

I reminded myself that I was out here for my son. The Taliban had not won. Al Qaeda did not destroy America or crush its spirit. It was my opportunity to do what I could to prove that to me, my son, and maybe even the world.

Breaking into my thoughts, I heard the pilot announce over the intercom that we were beginning our descent. We all looked out the windows. As we lost altitude, I could see in sharp detail the white and brown of the winter scene that was Kabul. There were many destroyed buildings, and I could see vehicles and tiny people moving about.

As we got closer to the ground, I saw the true destruction and decay. Bombed planes lined one side of the runway and the other side was littered with the carcasses of old planes that had been cannibalized for parts. The runway tarmac was rough, patched but functional.

The airport terminal was in terrible condition. The windows were blown out and half of the building was destroyed. The usual airport accommodations were nowhere to be seen—no luggage carriers, no food-service trucks, and certainly no emergency vehicles or personnel. And so I thought, *this is what an airport in a war zone looks like.* Various uniformed soldiers were walking about, carrying Kalashnikovs or AK-47s. I saw no American soldiers.

The terminal had no immigration booths to stamp our passports, no custom officers to inspect our bags, and no duty-free shops. It was the barest of buildings, with ragtag officials wandering around the dismal interior and hopeful-looking greeters carrying signs with names of organizations and expected passengers.

I saw an unkempt man holding a sign: "American Embassy." Those were beautiful words everywhere I went but especially in this new, strange, and frightening place. I told him I was with the embassy. He checked my name on his clipboard and told me to stand behind him.

Two other embassy staff besides me were arriving, including the Charge d'Affaires. Normally, someone of her rank, as the top person at the embassy, would have a special car and driver to greet her. This abnormality was the first sign that this embassy posting would not be like any others. Once we were together, we were escorted out a back door to identify our bags and load them into a dented, rusted, old truck. Then we headed to another vehicle with a hand-printed sign in the window reading "US Embassy." In the first of many acts of trust I would take in Afghanistan, I got in the vehicle that supposedly belonged to America. I was very much aware that I had just walked into a country where no official had stamped my passport.

Chapter 4

First Thoughts on Arriving

In Kabul at this time, the Afghan people did not resent us for being there. It was the beginning of February 2002, and the US military and State Department had been in the country only a few months. The Afghans were wary but full of hope—hope that they would be freed from the brutal rule of the Taliban; hope that the constant wars of the past thirty years would end; and hope that they could eat, sleep, and educate their children in peace. It was a time of hope for everyone. The international community hoped that we could lift these people out of their misery and into a new world order after generations of poverty and war. It felt like this was a moment to honor the humanity of the Afghan people, to honor their deep faith and their long-held, treasured traditions. It was also a time to show the world who we were as a people. The United States would combat the scourge of terrorism and free these exhausted people who had suffered for decades. In the process, we would be rooting out the terrorists who had planned the attacks of 9/11 on the United States.

In the beginning, I was struck by the poverty of Kabul and the beaten-down look of the people. But at the same time, I was in awe of the majesty of the mountains surrounding Kabul and surprised at the simple beauty of Afghanistan. It is a place of snow-capped mountains; rugged, handsome men; and secretive, strong women. They live, survive, and even thrive in the harshest of climates and conditions. Villages existed in harmony with nature and the people lived well off the land—that is, until outsiders came and destroyed so much of their land, peppering it with land mines. Afghanistan had ancient underground water irrigation systems, acres of almond and fruit groves, and mountainsides full of fat sheep—all before the foreigners came to make war on their land. And now, we were there.

And to this, I came wounded and angry at the world, unsure of how I would work in this complex, foreign culture.

It was with a great deal of humility and trepidation that I arrived in Kabul. I had the might of the US government behind me and an incredibly talented and committed team to work with me. This gave me courage and confidence in our programs and goals.

During my short stay there, I was to learn so much about Afghanistan. I had had little advance time in the States to do an in-depth study of the people and the land, and maybe that was not all bad. I arrived a bit confused about my life and sick at heart but also unbiased, with no preconceived impressions about this strange, enigmatic place. As I plunged into my work, I began to learn its secrets, see its beauty, abhor its horrors, and respect its resilience, unmatched by any other country in the region. I began to understand that the pride of the Afghan people was rooted in the fact that no foreign power had ever conquered their country, though many had tried, from Alexander the Great to Genghis Khan, the British, the Soviets, and now the Americans.

When I arrived, I couldn't help but wonder if our fate as Americans would differ from that of our predecessors throughout history. We were hopeful, not of conquering, but of liberating these proud people. There was a lot that I would wish to change about Afghanistan—the constant tribal fighting, the ethnic hatred, the incredible poverty, and the status of women. And I soon discovered that for those to change, the changes would need to come from within their culture. It could be no other way. Among themselves, they are—and have always been—free. Even the women, while lacking in many personal freedoms, carried a pride in the history of Afghanistan.

Chapter 5

The American Embassy in Kabul

We went straight to the American embassy from the airport on that cold day in February 2002 to check in. The arrangement was for all US diplomats to work at the embassy, but since there was very limited living space there, I needed to room outside of the compound, in downtown Kabul. This was a bit unusual given the threat for all civilians in the country, especially foreigners. In most countries, the American government provides housing either on the grounds of the embassy or in safe housing outside. But no one was in Kabul yet to arrange for housing, so I had to do it on my own. Hence my need to work with the NGOs we were funding to find room in their guesthouses or residences. On this trip, I arranged to stay at the Save the Children guesthouse, where I would go after checking in at the embassy.

The American embassy had the unkempt look of an abandoned building, which is what it had been since January 30, 1989, when it had last closed its doors prior to the onslaught of the civil war. The massive front doors were composed of ornate steel with shattered-glass inserts, and windswept debris fluttered on the neglected lawns. The grounds, though now overgrown, showed a history of tender care. Old beds of flowers were half-buried in the snow. I would later learn that the Afghans love their flowers and had cultivated beautiful rose gardens with well-tended lawns during times of peace.

In contrast to what I imagined the building once was, it was now a fortress of US military power, consisting of 150 marines and just us few fifteen or so diplomats. Although there were no modern security systems in place, it was still very intimidating. The perimeter walls were by no means up to the safety standards of 2002, and so the alternative was a show of overt might. On entering the dusty embassy grounds from the street, I was faced with two heavy-duty artillery machine guns facing right at me and manned by US marines. They meant business, intending to make sure that no one would be inclined to mess with them.

Every time a vehicle entered the driveway necessitating the opening and closing of the rather flimsy gates, it was immediately directed off to the right and down into a sandy area for a bomb search and dog inspection. All people without an embassy pass underwent a body search. I was spared this indignity as I had an American embassy badge from Pakistan, where I was living in my temporary quarters. It was immediately obvious to me that it was no small feat to get onto the embassy grounds. Once our vehicle was cleared, we drove around to the front entrance of the embassy, usually an imposing edifice, but here we were faced with those broken doors, smashed windows, and marines standing guard with their weapons. On first approach, this was quite daunting.

Far to the left of the embassy's front door on the grounds was a small memorial stone marker for Ambassador Adolph (Spike) Dubs, who had been assassinated on February 14, 1979, after being kidnapped in Kabul. Since then, no ambassador had replaced him. I was aware that I was walking not only on historical ground but also on hallowed ground. I already knew that Afghanistan was a land of unimaginable tragedy but was to learn that it was also one with an exotic Eastern history, full of wonder and untold drama.

Stepping inside the embassy building felt like stepping back in time. It had once had a grand entry with marble floors and a wide, ornate center stairway. The staircase went up one level and then split off to the left and right. The building had a regal look to it but was dirty. It was like a grand ole dame, grown old and neglected. This had once been an American embassy that presented itself with dignity and style before the world changed and required high-security doors, shatterproof windows, and metal detectors; it had been an embassy meant to invite visitors in, not keep them out.

To the right, just inside the front door, was a cubicle for a US marine guard, who served as much as a greeter and information clerk as a security guard. Beyond the marine's window was a weapons room and, next to that, a marine break room. I learned that when the break room was first opened, it had been like opening a time capsule. Back when the embassy closed in 1989, anything related to US national security had been either destroyed or taken with the departing staff. The break room, however, had simply been locked up. So when it was reopened, it still had the old newspapers, undrunk Cokes, and leftover napkins lying around. I was fascinated at the stories about these finds.

Now, the embassy was filled with US Marines. Normally, an American embassy will have ten to twelve American Marines assigned to it and hundreds of civilian staff. Here, it was the opposite, with about 150 Marines and only a dozen civilian diplomats, including everyone from the plumber up to the acting ambassador. The large rooms on the first floor, which might have been used for formal receptions in the 1960s, 70s and 80s, were now marine barracks. Peeking in, I saw rows of cots with a duffle bag stashed under each one. There was definitely no room at this inn for me.

As I went upstairs to see what would become my office, I took the branching stairs to the left and then went to the right into a small hallway. My office was the first on the left—along with about eight others. This entire setup was completely out of character for American embassies around the world. Usually, a separate room would be assigned for team leaders and cubicles for rank-and-file team members. Here, we each had a small space at a counter along the wall. Everyone was doing work on his or her lap since there was no room for personal desks and the counter space that ran below the wall of windows was too small for computers. There was a large center table for staff meetings. I could already feel that this was going to be an interesting and challenging setup in which to work.

I was greeted with enthusiasm by each person. They were obviously pleased to have our humanitarian office represented in country, and with their individual personalities peeking out, they began giving me tips for survival in this office working elbow to elbow. Everyone introduced him- or herself and identified what USAID office he or she represented. And so I began to learn the role that each person would play in our team approach in bringing in humanitarian assistance.

Since we were a bare-bones operation, everyone's role was critical. We would work as a unique unit inside the larger team of the USAID mission, which then fit inside the yet larger team of the full embassy. As this was my first day walking in, I got only quick introductions in my office and around the embassy. These were people I would come to care about, laugh with, and agonize with as each of us struggled to do our jobs and develop our programs. This was the moment I began to feel I had arrived, if only for this short three-day stay while I scoped out options for bringing in my full team permanently from Pakistan.

The physical limitations were apparent immediately. The room was small, maybe twelve feet by sixteen feet, with windows across the exterior wall above the counters. The floor was dusty, well-worn hardwood, and the interior walls were bare except for a few regional and country maps. There was a bulletin board with thumbtacked notices, the signs of US bureaucracy even here in Kabul—how to take sick leave, employee rights, and tax forms. There was comfort in seeing these familiar trappings that spoke of home and normalcy and routine bureaucratic procedures. The windows were cracked, and dust was everywhere. There were no telephones that worked, so we had to go from office to office to talk to our colleagues. All telecommunications equipment for talking with Washington was behind locked doors through which only security-cleared Americans were allowed. I was given the lock combinations for entry to this secured hallway. The codes had to be memorized, never written down, and *every* door inside that hallway had its own combination code. This became a daily mental challenge for me, rather like those games that exercise the brain to maintain optimal function. The lock combinations were changed monthly, effectively making moving around inside the embassy our own brainteaser.

My brain was spinning on this first day of introductions to life in Kabul. As with most things, time and repetition produce a sense of normalcy even in the strangest of circumstances. On this visit, my goal was to get an overview of working conditions, check communications provided by the embassy, assess the living conditions, and meet key people both at the embassy and outside within our NGO partners. I had a full three days in Afghanistan before catching the next UN flight back to Islamabad. I didn't know it then, but it was to be another six weeks before I would return to Kabul, and a lot would happen before then.

Chapter 6

No Room in Heaven

As noted, the embassy was overcrowded with marines and State Department staff essential to its function. Our team, while critical to Afghanistan, was not critical to the embassy.

Hence, I learned that when I traveled to Kabul, I needed to make my own arrangements to stay in downtown Kabul. On this trip, I was staying at the Save the Children guesthouse. It was a large, old, white colonial house with five or six bedrooms, surprisingly similar to what one might see in rural New England. And it was functional to a point. A cook provided breakfast and dinner. The house was approved as a living space by the security staff at the embassy and by the home office in Washington. While I wasn't sure anyone had actually seen the place and inspected it for safety, its location was known.

I usually met interesting people when staying in a group house. During dinner I met two women who would be sharing a room with me, a gender specialist and a child development specialist. The dinner table was a great place to network, to get to know the staff of our partner organization, and to learn more about the programs they were implementing with our money. Aside from my roommates for the night, the other guest in the house was a water engineer who had recently arrived in Kabul to assess and plan for the coming summer's water needs. The conversation was lively and informative.

Jenny, the gender specialist, spoke of her work with the women of Kabul.

"Sue, Save the Children is so grateful for the funding from OFDA. I'm meeting today with a women's group that has been kept in hiding for the many years of Taliban rule. They are led by a doctor who has been trying desperately to assist them with their maternal health care."

I was immediately interested in hearing more of what Jenny had to say. "Please update me," I told her. "I do get the reports, but I love being able to hear about the programs and the work with the people directly involved."

"That's great. I have some ideas that I want to float by you as possible extensions to our program and, if you have time tonight, would love to use this opportunity to talk. Looks like it's a good opportunity for both of us. I'm so glad Save the Children could host you tonight."

I asked, "What are your thoughts first on the existing program? How are the women responding to you as a Westerner? Our office is very concerned about the health and well-being of the Afghan women given the years of suffering and neglect that they've experienced."

"They are good, so brave, and the doctor who leads the group is committed to making their lives better and childbirth safer," Jenny said. "Dr. Azara studied medicine during the time the Soviets were in Afghanistan. Her education is a bit behind the latest medical practice, but she has the basics, and most importantly, she wants to learn more. We are offering a general medical ob/gyn review course that is being developed in the States. My goal on this visit to Kabul is to get a good understanding of what is needed and what the baseline of knowledge currently is. If their English is good enough, I have access to some medical books that I can send out from the States. If we can begin to build a library for them, it will be useful beyond our program and to other physicians. I'll be here for another six weeks to meet with our local female staff and review the entire program."

"Great!" I replied. "If possible, I'd like to schedule an opportunity to sit in on one of your women's group meetings. I'm only in Kabul for three days this time, but our office plan is to have our team move here within the next month. I have my business card with all my contact information. Please contact me and we can see what we can arrange. As usual, I will have some restrictions on where I can go, but right now, I am allowed to plan meetings with advance notice to the embassy for security. And after looking at the current program, I'd be happy to discuss a follow-on or expanded programing. We will be here with more funding for civilian needs. Let's talk more."

I then turned to Sarah, the Save the Children's child specialist. Sarah was a beautiful young woman in her mid-twenties with a mop of thick, curly, red hair. I immediately liked her ready smile and imagined how the children would be drawn to her youth and radiating joy. "Sarah, how is your program going?" I asked. "Are you able to get the young kids into the center you're setting up?"

"If there is food, they'll come," Sarah laughingly replied. "We try to provide a snack along with our outreach program. The parents are very leery of us, and it's a struggle to get their fathers to approve their coming to a Western-run school. The extra meal provided each day is a big help to the families, and so they send the children. Unfortunately, our attendance is predominantly boys, but we're really working on getting girls into the program. We have rented two separate buildings so the parents will be assured that the girls will not mix with the boys. It is an extra expense but unfortunately necessary," Sarah explained.

"I completely understand, and you will just need to explain the extra expense in your monthly report," I replied. "We do recognize the reality of working here, and one reason for our team's coming into country will be to further understand the cultural and religious constraints so that we can be more convincing in explaining expenses back to Washington."

"Do you think you can visit with us at our center?" Sarah asked. "It should be fully functional in two more months. If you or a program officer can visit, we would love it." I could see that she was quite enthusiastic about her outreach to the children and made a note to visit once we established our permanent office.

I was also quite curious about the work of the water engineer. The water situation in Kabul and much of Afghanistan was critical, and I knew our head office was especially interested in supporting more water programs. I turned to Jeff, sitting across from me, and asked, "Jeff, can you tell me a little about what you've been finding here?"

Jeff was a wiry older man, maybe in his fifties. He looked well-worn from years in the field but was a highly experienced water engineer who knew the lay of the land in undeveloped countries. He was pleased to get his chance to pitch his program directly to me as one of his program's primary donors. "The entire water system in Kabul is shot to hell," he replied, without preamble. "So much of it has been destroyed. The years of war have taken a terrible toll on all the infrastructure, especially in Kabul. Almost all the destruction you see here was at the hands of the rival factions within Afghanistan. I am just finishing up a study of the existing water system, such as it is. I know there is need of some major repair work to be done. Most of this will be outside of your office's scope of work. I expect to meet with the World Bank in the next few weeks to talk to them about their plans for assisting in a major city water system repair. But for now, we are trying to set up community wells and chlorination schedules to increase the quantity and quality of the water. I am particularly concerned about the summer, the hot and dry season. The potable water needs will increase, and right now the situation doesn't look good."

"I have a water engineer in DC who is available for consultation and who will review your project, so make sure that Save's home office calls him," I said. "Do you have his name?"

Jeff nodded and continued. "We are just beginning to do outreach to some of the villages around Kabul. They're in dire straits also. The pressure is to get clean water to everyone before summer when the potential for cholera or diarrhea is high. I hope to have my survey done by mid-March, and I will have both the team here and the one in Washington talk to you and your office."

"That's great. The timing should be good for planning on summer funding."

I was struck at how committed our partners were and the quality of staff who were working in Afghanistan. As I looked around the table I felt such gratitude and reassurance that these would be our partners in programs. If Sarah, Jenny, and Jeff were representative of the international staff in Kabul, I had high expectations of providing good programs to assist the civilian population.

As valuable and interesting as this conversation was, I was tired. The next day was going to be a full one starting very early. I excused myself from the table and headed off to bed.

The winter nights in Kabul were piercingly cold. There was no working central heating in the building. Instead, small, portable kerosene heaters were placed throughout the house. The one in my bedroom, unfortunately had a small leak of kerosene, which almost asphyxiated me and left me with a headache in the morning. Before realizing about the lead, I had chosen to sleep next to it for warmth, but I could not turn my face toward it. I got up sometime during the night to turn it off because I couldn't stand the smell and truly feared getting sick. In the morning I knew I would feel too nauseated to eat breakfast.

I reminded myself that this was considered five-star lodging in Kabul even though it had no central heating, no private rooms, and no private bathrooms. Most of these limitations only required minimal accommodations, but the lack of a functioning telephone to provide direct communication with the embassy concerned me.

During the day I carried a two-way radio issued by the marines as my only means of contacting the embassy. But these radios were not supposed to be taken outside the embassy compound overnight. They had been specifically programmed for the marines and the American embassy, so anyone with access to them was privy to the stilted, but open, conversations between Americans. I was desperate to have some kind of communication with the embassy and felt frustrated by this rule. I wanted to be able to give the embassy my location if it changed or check in for any updates on surrounding conditions. At that time there were very few local land line telephones and no cell phone service. Without my embassy-issued radio, I had no means of conveying any changes in my status to my American colleagues. I felt very alone and vulnerable without the radio. Even so, I was always very careful to return it to the marines each night. The one backup I had was my Washington-issued satellite phone (not a local or international cell phone) that I could use to call for help to my US office thousands of miles away. If necessary, the triangulation from me to Washington and then from Washington to the embassy in Kabul was available for critical information exchange at night but could take up to fifteen minutes to complete. This was frustrating since I was located only a few miles from the embassy in another part of Kabul. I was looking forward to the day when we would be assigned a room at the embassy to sleep in. My life would be so much easier and safer then. Still, I was glad to have this Save the Children guesthouse available to me now.

On this particular stay, I had forgotten to return my marine radio to the embassy before leaving the compound. By the time I realized my error, I had already been dropped off at the guesthouse and had no way of going back to the American embassy. My only course was to keep the radio secured with me all night, so I slept with it under the covers of my bed—another concern for me along with those kerosene fumes. I was essentially stranded without a vehicle overnight since we were not allowed to keep an unsecured vehicle off the embassy compound at night because it posed too big a risk. The vehicle could be tampered with: an explosive device might be attached to it. I had been trained to inspect my vehicle prior to getting in, but I was no expert, nor did I have a bomb-sniffing dog with me. At night, under cover of darkness, a terrorist could hide a bomb deep in the engine where I wouldn't find it, or he could implant a timed device that could be set off once the vehicle was at the embassy. It was for this reason that I could not keep a vehicle at night.

When I took the vehicle in the daytime, I had to follow strict procedures for signing it out. I had to register my destination, the time of use, and my expected time of return. I was also required to list all personnel who traveled with me. I understood that it was essential to follow these procedures. Amid all the chaos, the rules and regulations were important. I knew that with limited protection in the high-risk environment, these rules could save lives.

And so another critical safety skill in Afghanistan was knowing how to communicate on a two-way, handheld radio. We were all given call signs, which were considered classified information and changed every two to three months for security. This meant that I had to memorize the code names of people and places, as we were not allowed to use real names or locations over the open channels of the radios. We were also not allowed to carry this secured information in written form, like a telephone book of names. This meant I had to learn the real names of the people I met, their function at the embassy, and then their code names. Without this knowledge, I could not talk with the embassy staff when I was off site. There was nothing like the feeling of isolation when I couldn't call for assistance in any foreign country but especially in this dangerous place.

The protocol when calling using the radio was a bit like a second language. For all movements or changes in my schedule, I needed to call over the radio to the marine guards at the gate to notify them. The security at the embassy was tight. There were certainly concerns of terrorist activities. All vehicle approach to the gates was tightly regulated for fear of a hostile vehicle loaded with explosives ramming the gates, as had happened in other key locations around Kabul. Hence, we were required to call in our approach to the embassy gates to ensure that we were greeted with *silent* machine guns stationed at the main gate.

My call sign was Jade. I liked its sound. The short, abrupt word was easy to hear and got my attention when the radio crackled.

Heaven was the code name for the American embassy. Radio-speak was short, covert, and purposely vague to give any hostile listener, if there was one—and there usually was—as little information as possible about who was traveling where and when. A typical conversation would go like this:

"Jade, Jade, this is Heaven, over."

"Heaven, this is Jade, over."

"Jade, you are needed back at Heaven immediately. Over."

"Roger that, Jade returning immediately. Over." I did not ask why, nor did I request ten more minutes out. I responded immediately in the affirmative to a direct order. Military personnel understood this, but often civilians would ask questions. We learned not to question but to respond immediately to direct orders such as these.

When approaching the gates at the embassy, I would radio in and say:

"First Base, First Base (this was the code name for the guard position at the front gate), this is Jade approaching Heaven in a white four-door SUV with three paks (passengers). I am twenty seconds out. Request permission to enter. Over."

"Jade, this is First Base, you are cleared to enter. Over."

Or they might say, "Jade, this is First Base, you must drive around for a second approach. Over."

Again, I was not allowed to chit-chat or ask why I couldn't come directly in. Instead I would reply, "Roger that. Jade out."

These few but very important words ensured the safety of the personnel guarding the gates and that the marines would not mistake a vehicle as that of a hostile intruder. It meant the gates of Heaven would open in twenty seconds and let our vehicle through in a smooth approach. The guards would prepare for quick access as the gates opened and shut behind me.

It was a slick, if primitive, operation and it worked. I wasn't shot, and the marines always smiled as I entered.

Sleeping off site from the embassy did have some advantages. I found I had increased freedom of movement, but this was countered with being exposed to higher risks. I got caught up in one of those high-risk situations early one morning on this trip into Kabul.

It was about six thirty on a frigid, snowy morning in Kabul in February 2002. I was overnighting in downtown Kabul at the Save the Children guesthouse. A car and driver had been loaned to me by another partner NGO, and the driver was to pick me up and take me back to my office at the American embassy in the morning. I had been given the driver's name and a description of the car for identification. With limited language skills and the high risk of being kidnapped, having all the basic physical descriptive information was critical before I got into any car with an unknown man. It was most certainly not like catching a taxi in any American city, where one trusts that vetting has been done and general safety is assured. I was a woman waiting alone on the street, a very unusual sight in Kabul. At 6:29, I went outside in the dark morning to watch for my car. The snow was falling and the dawn was trying to break through a thickly overcast sky. There was an eerie, otherworldly feeling to the morning. I didn't want to be standing alone on this desolate side street for too long. I made a point of being punctual.

A rusty, four-door sedan of indeterminate age stopped. It was, as best I could tell, a dark red Toyota with the paper logo of International Medical Corps NGO taped to the right front window. My travel arrangements were a patched-together scheme that covered my logistical needs over these three days including sleeping at one NGO's guesthouse, borrowing a car from another NGO, and meeting with multiple other NGOs headquartered throughout the city. These kind of haphazard, loose arrangements are exactly what drive security specialists crazy. Regardless, while the car appeared to be the one I expected, when I looked in, I saw that the driver was not. I was told it would be a gray-haired man with a beard, about fifty years old, and a bit chubby. This driver was small in stature and much younger, and he had no beard. He was garbed in the familiar *shamal kamez* and smelled of early morning coffee and the familiar garlic and spices used in the local cooking. When I questioned him about his identity, he told me in broken English, "I am Mohammed, nephew of Ahmed. Ahmed sick. I drive today." He then said, "Get in." Even giving a lot of space for language limitations, this sounded rude. He also seemed rather cocky and brash. Maybe it was just his youth and the rush of power he got from being behind the wheel of a car, which was a status symbol in Kabul. Or his curtness could have reflected his lack of experience working with a Western woman. Whatever, I just did not feel good about jumping in the car at his command.

I started thinking, *Where have I heard that story line about being a substitute driver before?* I was anxious about this pick-up. It gave me the creeps. Our security trainers back in Washington always told us to trust our guts. If you get a bad feeling, listen to it. And then I remembered: in the news that January, there had been a report about the recent, tragic kidnapping of *New York Times* journalist Daniel Pearl in Karachi, Pakistan. Reports indicated that he had been given a similar excuse for a substitute driver when he entered his car that morning. He was never seen alive again. I started to think about what I should do. The dangers of living in Afghanistan came crashing in on me. I studied him, trying to make up my mind and knowing that if I made the wrong decision, it could be fatal.

Standing on the street that morning, facing the unknown driver, I remembered my radio. I was grateful for my error in keeping it with me. I had to make a decision: Go with him or not. The problem was, I had no way to let the embassy know if I changed my plans. It was the middle of the night in Washington, and I dreaded waking the person on call to request that he call the American embassy in Kabul with a message from me. So I took out the radio. The battery had died overnight, but the driver didn't know that. I asked for his name and his driver's license (as if I could read it), then went to the back of the vehicle to see his license plate. I told him that because of the driver change, I had to call in the new information to my supervisor at the embassy. Then I pretended to call, making a great show of saying his name and license number and my location. When I was done, I looked at the driver and with great gravity told him, "Now the US embassy knows who you are, what vehicle you are driving, and where I am. If I am not at the embassy gates in fifteen minutes, they will come get you." It sounded ominous, as I meant for it to.

With my heart pounding, I got into the car, said a silent prayer for my safety, and directed the driver to proceed. Never did those two machine guns look as good to me as when I arrived back at the embassy—Heaven, indeed.

I returned the radio with my apologies for keeping it with me all night, and I explained how I had used it for my safe return that morning. Since the battery was dead and I had kept it on me at all times, I was not reprimanded.

Still, the incident marked a significant turning point for me. I decided that the security risk was too great for me, or anyone else on my team, to stay out in the city with rotating drivers, unsecured vehicles, and street-side pickups without proper communications. I had stretched security to its limit. I had another decision to make. The safety of my team and myself was my primary responsibility as the team leader. This was partly why I was on this trip to Kabul. I needed to assess the situation until we could be accommodated at the embassy compound, which was not to happen for another month.

I left Kabul after my planned three days to return to Islamabad, to our temporary team base, with no plans to return until safer sleeping arrangements could be made. The American embassy in Kabul had to make room for us in Heaven.

Chapter 7

Living in Islamabad and a Bombing at Church

Living in Islamabad was a pleasure compared to the depressing destruction, isolation, and tension of Kabul. Islamabad has wide, paved streets divided with green gardens and walking paths down the middle, separating traffic on the main roads. There are lots of large evergreen trees and manicured grassy squares that give the feeling of peace and tranquillity. People live in blocks, identified by systematic addresses like House 23, Block K, Zone 5. With a good city map, it all made sense. I was surprised by its organization, space, and beauty.

In the evenings, I could go outside in our guesthouse garden and enjoy the fresh air, cool breezes, and birds chirping. All were complements to this good city planning. When I made appointments to go out, I liked that I could figure out the location of my destination given the rather boring, but very functional, address system. There were no flowery names of streets, but the unromantic, mechanical, numerical system worked. Shops were plentiful and colorful, loaded with beautiful, silk shawal kamez for women. The sidewalks offered up itinerant salesmen selling pearls, silk scarves, or the occasional luxury of gold jewelry. I never bought the gold, so I am not sure if it was real, but the pearl salesman dramatically demonstrated the authenticity of the pearls by scraping them on the cement sidewalks to show they were real. I bought the explanation and the pearls as gifts for family back home. Fresh fruit markets stood on many corners and in the numerous little strip malls. The fruits and vegetables were fresh and tasty, having been grown locally or in the region. The people were generally friendly, spoke good English, and were polite. I found a Chinese massage parlor where, for the price of fifteen dollars, I could get a good, one-hour massage. I liked Islamabad.

This government city, built in the early fifties for the new country of Pakistan, was a surprisingly beautiful city. It had broken off from India during a bloody war that wrenched families and communities apart and resulted in much death and destruction in the process. But the city of Islamabad, meaning "the home of Islam," seemed to put great effort in trying to create a new beginning for the country in its architectural beauty and preservation of the natural green spaces.

The government buildings were modern and elegant in style, usually made of white granite in clean, modern lines with a touch of the Orient and Arabic calligraphy. In March, for the Prophet Muhammad's birthday, the buildings were draped in thousands of white and green lights. They looked delicate and elegant at night, rather like wedding cakes richly decorated with multiple loops of colored frosting. Both traffic and people were sparse, unlike the bustling neighboring city of Rawalpindi. It was a real treat to drive or walk around the city, especially near the government center at night to see the lights, much like we do in the United States at Christmastime.

Islamabad, like Washington, DC, was designed to impress visiting dignitaries. The police were nattily dressed, and the traffic lights worked. When I attended government meetings, the security and check-in system was well known to me. I was usually dropped off outside a gated area and was left to my own devices to walk into a compound and find the correct building. "Excuse me, can you direct me to the director for urban development's office?" I would ask.

"Madam, I don't know that office. Wait one moment and I will call the central switchboard for directions," the guard at the gate often responded. They usually only knew the locations of "the big guys," as they like to call the higher-ups. "Ah, I have found it," the guard said as he came out of his gatehouse after a brief phone conversation. "It is in the third building on the left, on the second floor. Someone at the building will direct you when you check in. May I see your identification before you proceed from here?"

I had this ready at hand, knowing it would be requested. "Here is my American embassy badge and my business card," I said. "You may keep my business card here, but I must have my ID badge back." This was another security requirement. There was always the concern that someone could copy our badges, so we were not allowed to leave them with anyone.

"Madam, I must keep your ID here at the gate and will return it to you when you leave," the guard responded.

My routine rejoinder to this was, "Sorry, I cannot leave my badge. Please keep my business card only." I would add, "I'm sorry, but it is a rule at my embassy, and I will have to miss my appointment if it is absolutely necessary." This was usually accepted as the request to keep my ID was only a token attempt, probably a low-level government effort to gain copies. I was seldom challenged on this point. Hence, I was always overtly polite but very firm on the need to have my embassy badge returned to me.

At the designated building, the admittance procedure was repeated and I was directed to walk up to the office on the second floor. I was grateful for first- or second-floor offices, as the buildings were large, hot, and dark inside, belying the light and airy appearance from outside. Elevators were always rather iffy, so I avoided them if at all possible.

The government complexes resembled those in India—not a point to be made as Pakistan did not like being compared to its larger, more prosperous neighbor in any way. But still, the Pakistanis were, like Indians, students of the old English colonial training and thus produced government structures that were much the same in function and in physical organization. Interiors of the buildings usually consisted of long, poorly lit, wide hallways with a plethora of dark, mahogany doors on either side. Every office had an anteroom where the secretary sat, and this is where the third-tier check took place. "May I see your ID, please?" the secretary would ask.

"Yes, here you are, but I will need my badge back," I would reply. "Here are two business cards, one for your files and one for the director." I knew this routine exactly. The next step in the dance of a prestige-laden protocol was for me to wait. Waiting was part of showing how busy the director was no matter when I arrived, be it fifteen minutes early or one minute early. Waiting was to be expected. I'd sit on either hard, wooden folding chairs or overstuffed, dark velvet chairs depending on the rank of the person I was meeting with. I preferred the wooden folding chairs because they were cooler and cleaner feeling.

"Would you like a cup of tea or water?" the secretary would ask, another repeated ritual at every government office.

"Thank you, I will have a cup of tea." And then, after the prerequisite short wait, I would be allowed into the main office and begin my business for that meeting.

The large section of the city located behind the federal government buildings in Islamabad is protected and allocated for all embassies. It is called the Diplomatic Enclave and, when I was there, had only a few controlled access roads with checkpoints where twenty-four-hour guards screened and recorded the identifications of visitors, destinations, and vehicles for everyone entering. Non-embassy cars were thoroughly inspected as a precaution against terrorism. Because of these security measures, we all felt quite safe within the Diplomatic Enclave.

After a few weeks, the small team that was to go into Afghanistan was still with me in Islamabad. Like me, their trips into Afghanistan had been only for a few days at a time. Since we were now stuck in Islamabad until safer living arrangements could be made for us in Kabul, we all worked from the American embassy there and coordinated our movements with either the Pakistan government as needed or just internally. The embassy had very limited space for our Afghanistan operations. While we had been graciously received and the embassy staff were supportive of our work, it really did not concern them as their work focused on Pakistan and ours on Afghanistan. Our actual office space was very tight, but the embassy did provide us with some of our critical needs. We had access to briefing rooms, classified computers, and secure telephone lines back to Washington.

Our team tried to be as little of a burden on this embassy in Islamabad as possible by using our own Washington-issued laptops and cell phones. We hired our own drivers and rental cars so as to not overtax the embassy's motor pool. Our drivers took us to and from work daily. We lived in a guesthouse on one of Islamabad's green squares, where we also ate most of our meals. We were not restricted in our travel after hours around Islamabad. In fact, Pakistan was still a family posting for US diplomats who could bring their wives and children to live with them on their two-year assignments. The atmosphere was cautious and observant but not tense or hostile. Children were present at embassy gatherings, which was such a pleasure. Families brought with them feelings of a normal community and home when on a foreign assignment. Such was the case in Islamabad. During these times of seeing others with spouses and families, it was hard not to feel a yearning for my own family. I would connect with people and think, *Hmm, wouldn't Mike like John* or *look at that cute baby.* Sometimes the moments would cut like a knife to my heart, and at other times, I just felt my distance from my family and a developing autonomy. It was a bit surprising and confusing to me how I was grounding myself in this new assignment. Thankfully, work was all consuming most of the time, and therefore, there was little time to brood over my loneliness or rethink who I was and how I was connected to family and friends back home.

In March of 2002, we provided the majority of our services for Afghanistan from this safer, more hospitable location. Our partners working in Afghanistan had offices in Islamabad also, which made it easy to coordinate with them. Their Afghan staff reported to them, and we met regularly with these partners about their activities and assessments of the ongoing humanitarian needs. My team stayed informed on the vulnerable population in Afghanistan and updated Washington daily. Our criterion for assistance was solely the need of the civilians, wherever and whoever that might be. We worked hard to qualify our recipients for aid and to make sure that we did not provide assistance to any combatants. Our days consisted of meeting with various NGOs to learn of their activities in Afghanistan, listening to their assessments of life in Afghanistan, and planning future programs and costs as we looked toward the months ahead. Of course, at that time, everything was critical. Conditions in Afghanistan were very bad. Another important part of my workday was meeting and coordinating with other donor organizations such as the UN, the European Union, the Japanese relief organization, the Australian relief organization, and so on. It was so important that we, as donors, coordinated to make sure that our money was used effectively and reached the most vulnerable people in Afghanistan. We felt the disadvantage of having to work outside the country. It was like trying to figure out what a family member living in another state needed without being able to visit them. We lived and worked while waiting for authorities in Washington— the State Department and the Pentagon—to work out on how to best and most safely get us into Afghanistan. And so, our stay in Islamabad became a waiting game. The needs of the Afghans were immediate and could not wait for us to come to Kabul.

As the days went by, a routine was established. Given the comfortable housing and relative control of my workweek, I began to feel settled in and decided to attend church one Sunday. I learned there was a community church somewhere inside the Diplomatic Enclave and asked my driver to show me where it was after work one day. I wanted to see the church, time my way back to the guesthouse, and plan with the weekend driver for my pickup on Sunday.

The church itself was a surprise to me. It was a small building with white clapboard siding reminiscent of many American country churches. It was a nondenominational church sitting in the center of a grassy lot. I was instantly nostalgic for my American childhood experience of attending a small community church with family and friends, and I looked forward to attending church that weekend.

Sunday morning arrived bright and clear. It was a good day to go to church. This was something I missed being able to do in most foreign countries. I especially liked being able to attend services in English. I was surrounded by the Islamic culture, which I loved, but I was yearning for a touch of home, which, for me, included Sunday church.

As I got dressed on Sunday, I was in a good mood, looking forward to an opportunity for some much-needed spiritual sustenance in my life. It was what grounded me when I was faced with the many horrendous situations that challenged me on a daily basis. I would often question whether there was any goodness left in humankind. And here in Pakistan, I was at a point in my life where I was challenging everything. I had come off a number of years in the Balkans, where I worked with people traumatized from the Bosnian War. How could there be a God when I saw people of both the Christian and Muslim faiths brutalizing one another? Stories of unspeakable events were related to me in Bosnia and Kosovo that reinforced the inhuman behaviour of all sides directed toward the others. I was reeling from finding this inhumanity in so many countries around the world where I had worked and often found myself questioning my faith. And I was still struggling to get my footing after 9/11, when my son was inside the World Trade Center. I had really been thrown for a loop. And so, going to church was a routine I could relate to and relax into. I felt that I needed to continue this part of my life while it was available to me.

We had our daily team meeting that Sunday morning to review the plans for the coming week, and then I went upstairs to dress for church. Just as I was about to leave, the phone rang. It was Jim, my boss in Kabul. He was in charge of all the project activities for USAID and had questions about the armored vehicles my office was sending to Kabul. Jim had lots of thoughts on how the vehicles should be controlled, who should maintain them, under what budget these costs should be funded, and so on. Jim was a detail man, and he wanted to review everything. I watched the time tick by, but there was nothing I could do. If I had shared with him my plans for church, he probably would have told me to go on and call him when I got home, but it was an important call and I didn't want to delay his work at the embassy in Kabul. Besides, getting the armored cars into Kabul would accelerate our being able to move the team there to live and work on a full-time basis. Working out the details was definitely to our advantage.

By the time I got off the phone, it was fifteen minutes past the time that the church service was scheduled to start. Including the time for the drive, I wouldn't make it there until the service was ending. I went outside the house and canceled my waiting driver. I felt disappointed, and not very charitable toward Jim. I had wanted to go to church and needed that spiritual time.

A few minutes after discharging my driver, an emergency text message came in from the embassy: "All U.S. personnel are to stay in their residences until further notice." I wondered what was happening; a lockdown was never a good sign as it was usually prompted in response to a security event—a breach or an attack. My team and I hunkered down to wait for more information. We called the embassy to report that all the team was accounted for and gave our locations, as was protocol.

Soon, another text came in: the church had been attacked. Grenades had been thrown in through the windows at the congregation during the service that morning.

My heart stopped. I had desperately wanted to be sitting in those pews that morning. It certainly gave me pause to consider the conditions under which I was currently living. My need for caution in all I did just skyrocketed. As the day went by, information trickled in about the bombing at church and the number of people injured, including some fatalities. Many were American embassy colleagues. It was a difficult day.

I made a mental note to call Jim and thank him for keeping me on the phone that morning.

The next day, my Monday morning driver, Mohamed, arrived to pick me up. He was pale and shaking. He immediately asked me, "Did you go to church yesterday?" He had been in a panic, thinking that I had gone to church as planned and now might be injured, or worse.

"Miss Sue, you are well!" he said. "I cried all night for fear you were in the church and hurt. I told my wife, 'She is there' when I heard the news. Thanks be to Allah that you are okay. *Al humdala la, al humdala la* (thanks be to God, thanks be to God)," he said over and over, looking toward heaven with his hands clasped.

I could see that he wanted to hug me, but Islam did not allow him to. He settled for giving me a big smile and thanking Allah again and again throughout the day. As the day progressed, we got more news about the bombing. The wife of one of the American diplomats was killed and several others severely wounded, necessitating their being airlifted out of Pakistan for medical care.

The days that followed were tense, full of secret meetings. Every American embassy has a secured, controlled area that is for Americans with classified clearances only. In Islamabad, that area was in full use. There was much conjecture about who attacked the church and why and how it happened. I thought of the controlled access to the enclave. I only knew that I had been spared. The embassy was now on high alert, and there were discussions about the general safety of all Americans in Islamabad.

The spring of 2002 was the last time American diplomats' families lived in Islamabad. The final recommendation was for families with children to take them back to the United States.

Our work continued with heightened security and new rules for travel. Our team still lived in our local guesthouse and used our own drivers to travel around the city, but the tone had shifted. Nothing would be the same for Americans living in Islamabad.

Chapter 8

My Look-Alike

A few days after the bombing incident, I went out shopping. I wanted to get my life back to normal as much as possible. I walked into a nice carpet shop, and all the employees immediately stood up. The owner, wearing a tan shalwar kameez with a gray sportscoat over it, approached me. He had well-cut, slicked-back, dark brown hair and a trim beard. He swaggered toward me with his head held high to stretch his five-foot-six-inch frame. As he approached, he said quite loudly, "Good afternoon, Madam Ambassador." Wendy Chamberlin, a young, talented diplomat for the US government, had been in Pakistan for a few months. I turned, thinking she must have come in behind me. But she was not there. The shop was empty except for me and the shopkeepers. Perplexed, I looked at the man in some confusion. Until then, I had not been mistaken for her. I hadn't thought about our looking alike, even though we have some physical similarities, like hairstyle and color, height, weight, and similar age.

"Excuse me? No, no, I am not an ambassador," I corrected him.

"Oh, you do not want to be recognized, madam," he said a little quieter. "I am so sorry. I will not tell anyone you were here."

I was becoming alarmed. "No, really, I am not the ambassador," I stressed. And I added for good measure, "Anyone who might kidnap me will get nothing for me. I am just an American working here." I said this rather loudly on the off chance that his employees sitting in the back of the shop could understand English so he would not target me in the future for a handsome ransom, or worse. He saw my sideward glance towards them and motioned for his employees to retreat to their places on the floor.

Two far less-well-dressed men scurried to the back of the small shop next to mountains of dusty, folded carpets to drink their tea while sneaking looks at me.

"Do not worry, I will tell no one," the shopkeeper reiterated. "You can shop here in privacy. I will protect you. I like to get the business of Americans."

"I really am not the ambassador," I insisted.

"Okay, madam. You are not who you are." The owner winked at me.

"Yes, I am who I am, and I am *not* the American ambassador." I felt frustrated and not a little worried. As I thought of it, I knew that I kind of resembled the American ambassador but really was surprised at this mistaken identity. An ambassador can often be a target in many countries with a high price on his or her head. To counter this threat, our American ambassador traveled in an armored car with considerable protection. I had a rented car, a rented driver, and only my wits for protection when I was out and about.

With a secret smile, the shopkeeper said, "Yes, I understand. Can I offer you some tea? Do you want to look at a particular carpet?"

"No, thank you," I replied. "I will come back another time. I think I will go home now. Thank you again."

"Please come back soon, madam. We will have fine carpets to show you, just for you."

It was my first indication that, to Pakistanis, I looked just like the American ambassador in Pakistan who traveled, as noted, with significant protection, especially in the days following the bombing. Like me, Wendy Chamberlain had a short, blond bob haircut with bangs across her forehead. I wasn't her double, but for the general public who only had newspaper and internet images of the ambassador to go by, that similarity was enough for them to mistake us for each other. Since my work concentrated on Afghanistan, I did not have the opportunity to mingle with many Pakistanis, officials or otherwise, so I had not had this experience before.

The next time this identity mix-up happened was at the memorial service for the American woman killed at the church bombing. I was waiting outside the auditorium at the embassy to help greet and direct many of the foreign diplomats as they arrived for the service. A high official from the Pakistani government arrived a bit late. I was just about to go in when I saw his car approaching.

His driver quickly jumped out and opened the door for the official. "Madam Ambassador, you did not need to wait for me outside," said the dignitary. "I apologize for my lateness."

"It is no problem," I said, not bothering to correct him. "Now that you are here, the service will begin."

He was greatly relieved and full of himself that he had been greeted by the "ambassador." I had done my part for keeping good diplomatic relations on a very sad morning. I often wondered if he later noticed that the real ambassador was wearing something different than me.

Yet again it happened. I was at dinner in a restaurant with friends in Islamabad. As we finished ordering our meal, a woman came up to me from a nearby table and started to speak to me. I was perplexed as I didn't know who she was. Seeing my confusion, she quietly "reminded" me that she was China's teacher. The ambassador has a daughter named China. "I am not—" I began.

She didn't let me finish. "No, no, I will not take your time tonight as you are about to dine, but I just want to tell you how much we miss China in class," she said. It was about two weeks after the bombing, and the American children had been sent out of Pakistan.

"But I am not—" I said again. My friends around the table looked quite confused by this interruption and had no idea what was transpiring. I felt a little chagrined to be caught in this mistake again.

"I am so sorry for interrupting your evening. I will return to my table but only want to say that China was such a good student. She is missed both by me and her classmates." She scurried back to her table, sat down looking a bit excited, and started talking rather animatedly to her dinner companions. I could tell that she was proud of being able to chat with the

American "ambassador." As they left, she gave me a friendly little wave. I waved back and made a mental note to discuss this situation with the ambassador at our next security meeting. My friends thought it was quite funny when I explained what had happened. They all replied, "Ah, you *do* look like Ambassador Chamberlain," "Yes, I see it now," and "Oh, isn't this a strange coincidence."

Yes, I did need to discuss this with the ambassador.

I was worried. If I looked that much like the American ambassador to the Pakistanis, then I was at great risk of being kidnapped. I knew I had to follow through and report the events to the *real* American ambassador the next morning.

Ambassador Chamberlain and I met, with the senior team of American staff, daily at 7:00 a.m. in the "bubble," our nickname for the secured briefing room—a room with a round shell of soundproof, thick, plexiglass shaped over it. During our next meeting, I told the ambassador about the incidents. She expressed her concern but could offer nothing concrete to reassure me, nor did her security team. No one had a solution to the problem as this had not ever happened before.

Feeling a bit bold, I asked the ambassador if she would consider dying her hair darker, thereby creating a new appearance different from the blonde bob we shared. I guess I was thinking that she was the famous one, not me, and as such if her appearance changed, I would no longer be in danger. It was a quick thought at seven in the morning and not a good one.

She took less than a second to consider. "Sue, I outrank you," she replied. "I was here first, and I'm content with my hair. You dye *your* hair."

The room burst into laughter. I sat back in my chair and said, "Oh, I hadn't thought of that!"

I decided to write to my Washington office and ask for a brown wig as a security measure for when I moved about the city. I could just imagine their reaction.

My driver was quite amused that everyone thought he was driving the US ambassador. That amusement soon turned to concern when I explained that he had to be extra cautious. I instructed him to be on the lookout for anyone following us or for anyone coming too close at a stoplight. "You need to notice if any driver or car is acting suspiciously," I said.

He quickly lost his enjoyment of driving the "ambassador" as he considered the potential risks to him. The old adage in the field was that they shoot the driver and take the people in the back seat hostage, and he knew this. We were not equipped to handle a kidnapping attempt, and my driver certainly did not have a gun.

The wig never materialized. The next morning, I was called home to America for a family emergency.

Chapter 9

Emergency at Home

The morning after our wig meeting, I got a call from home at about six thirty in the morning my time. It was still dark, and I was not quite awake yet. A call that early in the morning could only mean one thing—a crisis. I answered the phone and, to my surprise, it was my husband. I knew it had to be something serious for him to be calling me so early in the morning. My first thoughts always went to my family—my children and my aging mother. But it was none of them. Mike had had a heart attack and was calling from his room in the cardiac intensive care unit at the Virginia Medical Center. Thank goodness it was Mike who called; at least I knew he was alive and could speak to me directly. In our twenty-three years of marriage, we had never faced any critical medical problems, so this sudden turn of events was stunning to me. We had always assumed that the one in danger was the person traveling. Our discussions of crisis seemed to center on what to do if something happened to me. I hadn't given great thought to the possibility of my family back home becoming the people in urgent need. The events of 9/11 brought home the potential for family being caught up in a critical event, but even following that, it felt like a one-in-a-million potential. And everyone was healthy, so given the potential for accidents, everyone always saw that the high risks were for me. But at this moment, Mike was in need. He said that he had called our oldest son, Eric, who lived in Atlanta, and he was on his way up to Virginia to be with him as we spoke. But right then, Mike was calling me. This was a serious scare as heart disease ran in his family. He assured me that he was in stable condition and under excellent medical care in the CICU. Eric was expected to arrive in a matter of hours.

I was in shock and groggy from the sudden early morning call. I immediately got up, dressed, and went downstairs in the guesthouse where my staff was gathering. At our morning staff meeting, I informed them about my husband. I couldn't think what to do. They were solicitous to me and asked what I needed. I didn't even know what to tell them other than that I would get back with them that afternoon. Later that morning, as I met in the bubble at the embassy, I also told the senior team members there.

"You must go home," the ambassador said.

"Do you need any medical care? Do you want something to calm you down?" asked John, the embassy doctor.

"We'll make travel arrangements immediately," Angela from staff support said. "I'll get the travel office on it immediately."

"You go back to the guesthouse and pack. Be ready to leave as soon as we get your travel arranged," the ambassador said. I felt wrapped in the caring support of my embassy family.

Many of us serving in overseas assignments are separated from loved ones. The instinctual response was to reach out to others in need since we all feared it could be us next time. We took care of one another. We were family.

I was completely undone by their kindness. There, surrounded by their loving care, it hit me: my husband, far away in America, was in the hospital in a cardiac care unit. It was then that I became really shaken by the news. Until then, I had been numb.

By that afternoon, I was on a plane heading home. I was met at each stop along the way by American embassy staff from each location in the Middle East until I hit Europe. They escorted me from flight to flight. The Islamabad American embassy travel team had done so much for me in just a few short hours.

I called the hospital from Islamabad before leaving so they could tell Mike that I was on my way and also to get an update on his condition. I then called again and again—from Karachi, from Dubai, from the plane over the Persian Gulf, from Geneva, from the plane over the Atlantic, from New York City, and finally when I landed in Washington. The nurses were getting a lesson in geography. I thought they must have pins tracking me on a map. When I finally arrived at the hospital, they told me it had been like a travel log. I had needed the reassurance all along the way that Mike was okay.

It was a grueling twenty-two-hour trip home through multiple time zones and with little rest. I was so relieved to see my husband that I finally collapsed in tears and *he* comforted *me*. I stayed with him in the hospital for that day, my suitcase by his bed. Later I went to our home in Washington where Mike was living while I was away and returned every day to the hospital until he was stabilized. After five days in intensive care, he was allowed to come home. I was also so grateful to Eric for coming up and staying with us for a few days until we felt sure that Mike was stable and I was rested enough from my long journey home.

I was in a haze. I called my team in Islamabad daily for updates and learned that they had been told to leave the country too. The security team at the embassy had made a judgment about the overall safety in Pakistan and decided to reduce the embassy footprint down to essential personnel only. Our work for Afghanistan was essential, but we were not essential to Pakistan, where we had been living and working. Every extra American was a liability in this newly hostile place following the church bombing. While it is usually necessary to keep key American personnel on site, in this case, our team was judged to be an additional liability for the embassy security apparatus. Consequently, my team had to pack up themselves and my remaining things and store them until we figured out our next steps. Our team had become homeless. They followed me back to Washington just a few days after I left.

We ended up working from Washington for the next four weeks while plans were made for us to return. Our goal was to get living arrangements inside of Afghanistan, which demanded intense negotiations with the personnel in Kabul and coordination with our security team in Washington. Each day after work, I went home to my husband. He continued to improve rapidly, but I needed to make some hard decisions. I had begun thinking more about what I wanted as Mike moved further out of danger. I did not want to be tied to home with an invalid husband. I just wasn't ready for that. I felt like a real shit for thinking like this but made myself face the possibility that Mike would need someone around all the time, living with him. This was such a sudden change in our lives: Mike, who was an international development specialist and had traveled extensively, now would be staying home on disability. Would I be required to stay home to take care of him? Love is a strange thing. I loved Mike, but I did not want to lose my life to his needs. In my work there seemed so little area for compromise. I either stayed home or I left. Mike and I discussed how our marriage would evolve. We had always been good about being open and honest with each other, and now that three or so weeks had passed since his heart attack, he was beginning to feel stronger. I could see improvement in him each day. I thought that, other than the new bottles of pills lining the bathroom shelf, our life could revert back to what it had been. Much of what he needed to do, he needed to be responsible for himself. I could not change his diet, change his exercise routine, or change his inner stress level. All of that was on him. Many wives would have felt they should be closely involved in the rehab process, and I was shocked and ashamed that I did not want to be involved. My wish and willingness to step aside at this moment weren't part of who I would have thought I was. I knew that we had to come to an understanding that worked for both of us and that I needed to feel at peace about his ability to take good care of himself. I also needed to be at peace with leaving him again. At this point, I was highly plugged into my Afghan work and the team I was working with. I was invested in the programs and wanted to follow through with them.

Mike and I discussed options for us both. We were still concerned about him being alone whenever I was able to leave, if in fact I did leave. We finally agreed to talk to his mother about coming to stay with him for a month or so if I returned overseas. As the days went by, it became more apparent that I would choose to return to Afghanistan. Mike was great about taking responsibility for his post cardiac rehab. He assured me that he would be fine and that I should go back. The team evacuation from Pakistan had provided this much-needed time at home, but now I was ready to return. My assignment would require me to remain in Afghanistan for another five months, taking me through August of 2002.

The Afghan team and I had been working daily in Washington on the funding sources and amounts for the ongoing programs in Afghanistan, as well as working on a solution to having as many of the team as possible return to Kabul. It was an enormous challenge to provide effective humanitarian services for the Afghans from seven thousand miles away. We needed to be closer at hand to respond to daily changes in conditions on the ground. Another component of our job was to verify that the programs being funded were being developed as planned and serving the people they were intended for. We monitored for any diversion of funds but also, and as importantly, monitored that those most in need were being served. It was impossible to do this from the remote location of Washington. We needed to be in Kabul.

We pressured Kabul to find room for us in Heaven. We were the only game in town for the US government in regard to bringing services to the civilians of Afghanistan. The government wanted a humanitarian face on its activities in the country, and yet we were still negotiating with the embassy in Kabul to share its tight living quarters.

The compromise and final decision was that our team would be cut in half and only four of us could go back—two women and two men. I made plans to leave again.

During these days of adjusting to Mike's new condition and working in Washington, we both communicated almost daily with the kids and with his mother. She was finally able to commit to coming to Washington to stay with him for a month. The kids were not pleased with my plans to return but had, after many years of my assignments overseas, come to accept that this was my work. They were very relieved to know that their grandmother would be at the house with Mike. In the end, I left with a heavy heart; with kids angry at me for leaving; and with Mary, my kind mother-in-law, surely disappointed in my leaving her son. This new person I was acknowledging and listening to who was leaving the country to work seven thousand miles away from a sick husband was a stranger to me.

Chapter 10

Living at the Embassy

I flew to Pakistan and gathered my things that had been hastily packed by my colleagues when they were forced to leave the country a few days after I left to go home to Mike. Everything was in storage at an embassy warehouse. The team had done such a good job of packing not just my things but all the documents, files, and equipment that we had in Pakistan. I needed to arrange for everything to be shipped into Kabul since we now had a place assigned inside the embassy grounds. Within a week, I was heading to Kabul. I was physically tired and emotionally drained from the frightening trip home to Mike in the hospital and then the difficult decision to leave again.

I again flew into the broken city with an even more trashed airport. Time does not serve any country well when at war. It had been about six weeks since my last trip to Kabul. More debris, decay, and ruin were overrunning the airport. I was not surprised, having seen it before. Even so, it was daunting to land among the refuse of war—broken, cannibalized, and abandoned airplanes lining the runway; broken windows in the terminal, and still no official immigration process to get passports stamped. But the embassy driver was familiar to me, and his handheld sign was a comfort. He checked me off his pickup list as having arrived, gathered the other American passengers from the UN flight, and headed toward my new home and office for the next five months.

Once there, with living and working full time at the embassy on a permanent basis, life entered a new routine—up at 6:00 a.m. and wash as able. I was living in a bunker underground.

The bunker consisted of three sleeping rooms. Each was about twelve by fifteen feet. We all shared the center hallway, which did triple duty as a cooking area, food storage, and dining space, though we only ate inside when the weather was bad. It was so dark and claustrophobic that dining inside was not an enjoyable experience. The men assigned to stay in the bunker were those sent out from Washington for a short-term assignment. The full-time civilian male staff lived with the marines in one of the large rooms in the embassy, sleeping on cots. Our two male staff members lived there and often spoke of it being reminiscent of their previous military days.

The women's room was able to accommodate both the long-term female staff and the occasional female staffer sent out from Washington. In total, twelve to fourteen of us usually lived in the bunker, all sharing one toilet. The plumber was our hero. He was a chubby, jeans overall-clad man from Mississippi who became the most important person to know. Even he required a security clearance and traveled with a diplomatic passport to work at the embassy. With so few civilians present, we all rubbed elbows, from the highest- to the lowest-ranking diplomats on a daily basis.

In the morning we stood in line in the hallway to use the bathroom. The hall was a poorly lit beige-tiled space of about six feet wide and twenty feet long. All of us were in our pajamas with toothbrushes in hand, shifting from foot to foot as we waited. On one cold April morning I found myself in line behind Zalmay Kalizad, President Bush's special representative to Afghanistan, who a few years later became one of the early ambassadors in Afghanistan. I had not met him personally but hesitated to extend myself at that moment since we were both in pajamas. The line formed in this dark, cold hallway of the bunker early each morning. We all stood on one side to allow for traffic flow, and it was usually very quiet. We were cold, barely awake, and probably all had bed-head hair and bad breath. We did not want to talk business while in this vulnerable state. Over many months, I spent time in line with some pretty interesting people who came out from Washington. The morning bathroom line was the great equalizer.

The other activity occurring simultaneously each morning in the hallway was breakfast. It was quite the communal spot. Dry cereal was usually the choice of the day as the cook did not arrive to start up the big black stove in the dark recess of the hallway until after nine o'clock. The early risers would stand against one wall eating their bowls of cereal as the late sleepers stood against the other, waiting for the bathroom.

Once I finally got into the bathroom, it was not a place of peace and tranquility. The walls were a dreary gray cement. At the far end from the door was the shower stall. It had one step up and closed with a rather nasty, old plastic shower curtain with pink flowers and green leaves on it. The toilet was on the left wall just next to the shower on a raised cement platform. With the lid down it served as a shelf for showering toiletries. To the right was a wooden cross strip with hooks in it to hold towels and clothing. The sad state of the room was finished off with a broken tiled floor. Next to the toilet was a small, rusty white metal sink attached to the wall with a small plastic shelf above for toothbrushes and hand soap. Above this was a small, scratched mirror. We spent as little as time as possible in this space. Still, this was the room that we all anxiously waited in line for each morning. In fact, it was one of only two communal toilets on the entire embassy grounds.

The bunker itself had two entrances, but the antiquated coal-burning stove and kitchen supplies blocked the back steps. So functionally, there was only one way in or out. That entrance was just next to the bathroom and made for a busy intersection. From outside coming in, we had to go down one flight of stairs to the underground level, stop and open the exterior door, and then turn right. The bathroom and shower were immediately to the right. The next room on the right was the women's sleeping room. On the left were two rooms, the first a kind of lounge/eating area that was sometimes used as an additional men's sleeping space, depending on the number of short-term staffers in from Washington. The second room on the left, directly across from the women's bedroom, was the permanent men's bedroom. Each room could sleep between six and eight people with our beds lined up against the walls. We lived out of our suitcases, which we stored under the beds. The beds were small, metal, and twin-sized. As I recall, the rooms were painted a pale green and had small, high windows that brought in the only natural light. We could not see out as the windows were set about eight feet up from the floor, which put them just above ground level on the outside. The bunker had a sloping roof line that stood about three feet above the ground. It was covered in grass, which made it almost unnoticeable from the outside but truly invisible from the air. It was my home for months until the embassy bought and shipped in some European campers and placed them on the embassy grounds.

Our emergency response team ranged in age from late twenties to mid-sixties. We all lived, ate, worked, and socialized together, as there was no other option. Tastes in music varied. The discomfort of dressing and undressing in tight group spaces could be a bit awkward, but we acclimated. We learned to give visual privacy as there was no physical privacy. It was not unusual to have three or four women in our room getting dressed while all turned toward the wall with clothing laid out on top of our beds. When done, I would walk out to the hallway with eyes cast downward and not look up until the door was shut.

The "kitchen," consisting of only the stove and supplies stored on the back stairs, was at the end of the dark hallway. When lit, the coal-burning stove polluted the air. As the temperatures warmed and the rainy season passed, we spent as little time underground as possible. The "cook" was one of the men who had originally worked as a gardener back in 1989 when the embassy had been shut down. I am not sure what qualified him to cook or how he was chosen except that he was just there when the troops and diplomats arrived in 2002. He was a tiny, older Afghan man about fifty years old who, in fact, knew little about cooking. Apparently, the most important qualification was that he had been cleared by our security team to be on the grounds and to feed us without fear that he would cause damage or *intentionally* poison us all. Once I got to know him, I found out that he was one of two faithful embassy employees who had come to work for thirteen years every day when it was closed. They tried to maintain the building and grounds as best they could. I don't think anyone was able to get inside the building, but they did what they could from outside. As it turned out, this man knew how to cook only brown soup and red soup. I got sick daily from the food. Taking the antidiarrheal medicine became routine. In the end, I had to stop eating anything that did not come out of an American box. I ate dry cereal, dry crackers, and on a good day, fresh fruit that I washed for myself. It was quite a diet; I lost weight quickly.

The few Afghans working in the embassy had to be escorted at all times. Even our faithful Afghan cook, who had ruled the embassy grounds over those thirteen years of American absence, had to be escorted if he came inside the building. I remember thinking, *Would I work every day without pay on the simple belief that the Americans would one day return?* When I asked why he did it, he said that felt he had a responsibility to do it. He told me, "I knew that Allah would make all right and he always takes care of me." It was the first of many times that I would be impressed by the simple faith of the good Afghan people. When he was finally paid his back wages, it made him quite a wealthy man, and we all celebrated his good fortune.

In contrast to our eating arrangements, the US marines were not allowed to eat anything cooked locally or that came from the local market for fear of being poisoned by terrorists. They ate the military's meals ready to eat, known as MREs. These meals were safe, hearty, and somewhat tasty, but most importantly they provided the needed calories for the marines. And if the meals began to taste like the plastic wrappers they came in, at least the marines knew they weren't being poisoned.

I deducted from this eating arrangement that we civilians were expendable, but the marines were not. Oddly, we did not complain about this. We each contributed five US dollars per day toward the food purchase. It was a bargain, even when my guts often lost the battle to retain it.

As I did a quick review of my life at that moment, I absorbed the fact that I was living in a bunker. I was svelte. I resided with approximately 150 US marines in fine condition, and I was one of only five or six women on the compound. There was plenty of room for ego trips here. Under such conditions, any woman looks better and better. I was often told by the marines that I was one of the best-looking women in Afghanistan. (To check that against reality, it's like telling your only grandson that he is your favorite grandson.) They never saw any other women. But it was nice to hear on days when I felt lonely or ugly or unkempt given the facilities available.

I was told that the summer would be very hot in the bunker, but it was still winter when I arrived and we were constantly cold. We slept in our sweat suits—all the better for midnight runs to the toilet and morning lineups with our colleagues. Dress code in the embassy was relaxed unless we had a meeting with a dignitary. I learned to dress and undress in relative haste and under cover if necessary. Luxury time in the bathroom was a thing of the past.

One day towards summer, as I stood brushing my teeth, I saw a new addition to the bathroom décor—flypaper hanging on each side of the mirror. It was curly, dull brown, sticky strips and already loaded with flies. They stuck there, languishing until dead. I watched the number of dead flies grow through the week until a new set of sticky strips was hung. I found out it was one of the women who had requested the flypaper from the States and was diligently changing it each week. When asked, she said that she could not stand battling the flies every time she used the toilet. We all agreed and were thankful. That was how it worked. Someone thought of something, asked for it to be brought out by the next short-term staffer coming in from Washington, and just like that, it appeared. Small mercies!

Office life offered its own set of challenges and entertainment. A couple of days after settling in to our new arrangements, I entered the office to find a young colleague hopping from desk to desk and corner to corner of the room. She spoke into her bulky satellite phone, saying, "Can you hear me now? Can you hear me now?" It was straight out of the TV commercial for a cell phone company back in the States. At best, the satellite service was sketchy, and at worst, it dropped so often that it made Morse code a more efficient communication method. My young colleague, jumping from place to place, served as a delightful form of acrobatic entertainment for the rest of us in the room.

Because we were a small group, I could go places in the embassy that would normally be off limits. One such place was the roof, where a lot of very sophisticated communications equipment was being installed. In this nascent embassy, the rules had not yet been developed that would have restricted this site from me. One day, a colleague and I were invited to come up to see the view of Kabul from the roof. A serious young marine escorted us and gave us a tour. Since I was not a communications technology buff, I didn't recognize the things on the roof. They only meant contact with the outside world to me. The means remained a mystery.

The view from the roof was amazing; I could see a wide swath of Kabul. Sadly, most of it had been destroyed. The gray, snow-capped mountains made for a somber backdrop to the destruction below. The fresh wounds of the city had come from the brutal fighting between the Taliban and the Northern Alliance militia, leaving the beautiful city's ancient castles, majestic homes, beautiful gardens, and busy streets in sad shambles. Long stretches of road were pockmarked with broken tarmac and littered debris. Buildings that hinted of a grand past, much like the American embassy had been, lined many streets. I had thought of Kabul and Afghanistan as very underdeveloped, but it was clear that Kabul had once been a great city. I could see crowded markets with few goods to sell. Still there were a lot of customers milling around. It took me a moment to notice that there were few women in the crowds. It always amazed me that men were the primary procurers of all things necessary for home and family in many Islamic countries with strict limitations on women's movement. The men even bought the women's clothes, including bras and underwear. Men also sold these items in the shops and kiosks on the streets, which always made me uncomfortable when I had to buy any intimate articles of clothing.

The city wore the tattered cloak of an old man, down on his luck. In the days to come, I would venture into Kabul and encounter more of its former beauty and its new scars. From that rooftop on that day, all I could see was a forlorn, broken cityscape.

After about ten weeks of living underground in the bunker, the embassy received its six new campers from Germany for permanent staff, each of which could accommodate two people.

I moved into a small one with Sandy, a woman from the State Department. Our tiny bedroom was tucked at the trailer-hitch end of the camper and surrounded by windows. It would have let in lots of natural light, but we seldom had the curtains open. The bedroom end sat directly on the side of the driveway facing the embassy. There was constant foot traffic around us, so for privacy, we always kept the curtains closed. Sometimes I felt like I was sleeping in a campground because there was so much chatter and commotion outside the windows. Of course, like most campers, it was not very soundproof, so I heard conversations outside quite clearly. Sometimes I could hear activity of the erotic kind in the camper next to me late at night. The singles scene was becoming quite active, and the combination of couples was always surprising. The pool of candidates was limited, producing unlikely partners. Often, it was a chance for a less attractive person to nab what might be considered a real catch in the outside world. Few of these liaisons lasted beyond the posting assignments, but it seemed that this pairing up was a comfort to those isolated in Kabul.

My loyal marines continued to reassure me that I was still among the most beautiful women in Afghanistan, and that was a comfort for me. I hugged the compliment to myself. There were lots of days when falling in the category of the top five beautiful women was heartening, especially after a long day of being sweaty and bounced along dirt roads. I did not feel the least bit pretty.

My camper was a haven and the only place where I could find some much cherished privacy after the weeks of close living quarters in the bunker. My roommate, Sandy, moved back to Washington after only a few weeks there, and from that time on I had the camper to myself. After so many months of crowded living conditions, it felt like I was living in luxury. I enjoyed this bit of small space for myself. It was a typical camper in style. The bedroom, at the back end, led into a very short hallway with tiny closets on either side. When I was sharing the camper, my roommate and I each took one side of the hall for our personal use. After she left, I had the luxury of claiming both sides of the hallway closets for myself. Sandy had worked in another area of the embassy, and we had not gotten close in her few short weeks with me. She was easy to live with and did her job, which was to set up a cafeteria contract with an Indian corporation to come in and provide meals for us. For this, she will forever live in my memory as a miracle worker. Within a matter of weeks, a prefab cafeteria was built and—voilá!—meals were prepared. Sandy was fondly remembered as a hero.

The camper hallway connected to a nonfunctioning kitchen with a square, booth-style table taking up the other end of the camper. There was a tiny bathroom, which also did not function since there was no running water. I used the bathroom as my makeup room and an overflow storage closet. It had the only mirror in the camper. The exit door was immediately next to the bathroom and across from the Pullman kitchen. I was well contained in my twelve-by-eight-foot home.

My home away from home comforted me. I worked efficiently when preparing for the day in my tight quarters. I found that I needed much less than I ever imagined when I was back in the States. The only thing I would have liked was running water for a functioning shower and toilet.

I still had to leave the camper and run out to the underground bunker, which was right behind me, to use its bathroom and shower. Otherwise, I was quite content and even entertained once in a while by hosting a rousing game of Uno at my table for four. We would have glasses of wine and enjoy a lively social evening.

Chapter 11

Mystique of the Burqa

The anonymous, invisible women of Kabul meandered in the teeming markets, their pleated ankle-length burqas swinging. Like pale blue ghosts, they floated by—phantoms in a poorly orchestrated dance. They seemed without personality, indistinguishable one from another.

"How does a child find his mother?" I asked Jamal, my driver one morning as we headed out for a meeting at one of the UN offices downtown.

"It is the shoes," Jamal says. "Children know their mothers by their shoes."

Jamal wove in and out of the chaotic Kabul traffic as he spoke. This was one of my early foray into downtown Kabul since moving into the embassy. Jamal was my driver and was quickly becoming one of my most important educators on the ways of life on the streets. He was about thirty years old with a short, uneven beard—left over from Taliban rule when all men were required to wear beards. The smells of fried foods, strong with onions and garlic, and of smoking tobacco were soaked into the rough cotton of his clothes, which were in need of a good wash. He seemed surprised when I hopped into the front seat of the car with him—already a faux pas. I had forgotten one of the lessons learned on the UN lawn, that I was not to be alone sitting in the front seat with an Afghan man or I'd risk being labeled a whore. The thought struck me, *I have not even gotten outside the embassy walls, yet already I've made this mistake.* I had much to learn.

Jamal began my next lesson in all things Afghan.

"We men know when a *young* woman walks by," Jamal went on. "The shoes will tell us and then we know to stand tall and be tough."

Flirting, Taliban style.

I began to get a hint of how men ascribed attributes to women beneath the veils. They built illusions of who stood beneath, illusions based on posture, stride, and shoes—the only visible distinguishing features of an otherwise concealed and anonymous person.

"A man knows if a woman is young or old by her shoes," he went on in his fantasies about each female. "I know if it is worth it to walk past this woman or not. I know if she is from a rich family or poor family. I know if she is healthy or not."

In this land of veiled women, the young and old alike found ways to compensate for their loss of uniqueness. The young mother was apt to wear distinctive shoes, such as with a buckle or clasp, so her child could find her in the marketplace. Once married, the colors of her shoes were usually relegated to black or brown for modesty's sake. A young girl found a way to look pretty when going out by wearing high heels and maybe even something really striking, such as red shoes. Teenaged boys (for even the Taliban could not control the hormones of sixteen-year-olds) found a bit of titillation in seeing toes—covered by socks—peeking out of shiny sandals. And the father, looking for a potential wife for his son, could spot a worthy candidate in expensive shoes.

I found myself looking at the feet of women with the intensity of someone with a foot fetish. Could a person live a whole lifetime knowing his neighbors only by their shoes?

Even though the American military were in Afghanistan assisting the populace to defeat the Taliban, it was not a clean-cut, done deal. Vestiges of Taliban rule persisted, from the more subtle issues within the privacy of homes to the more obvious rules, such as beards for men and burqas for women. Some households were run under the same strict guidelines as under the Taliban, where many behaviors did not change. Most importantly, the women didn't trust that the Taliban wouldn't come back one day and punish those who'd strayed from their restrictive dress codes and ways of life. Women stayed covered. It was the safest thing to do.

Jamal arrived on a later morning as we were heading out to another meeting in downtown Kabul. He sported a wide, shit-eating smile exposing neglected, nicotine-stained teeth and a tooth missing on the upper right side of his mouth.

"What's that smile about today?" I asked.

"Today is a windy day."

"What? Why does the wind make you so happy?" I asked.

"Madam, the wind moves the burqas against the women, and I can see their form." In his shyness, Jamal fairly swooned. "Allah makes the wind to blow. I must look where I am going. This brings an unexpected pleasure."

I was caught up in his explanation. Was this innocence to be celebrated, or was it a travesty of the modesty demanded of the women? Jamal's imagination was fed by the most innocuous of things—the wind. He took a simple joy from looking at a woman's form against the windblown burqas.

My initial thought was, *How cute and funny.* But then I thought of the enforced wearing of the burqas that stripped women of their individuality and freedom of expression. Merely by the wind pushing or lifting her burqa against her body, she excited the men looking at her. It was a small violation without her knowledge or permission and was outside of her control. A free woman could choose to dress for effect, but Afghan women had no choice and furthermore were blamed for being provocative if the wind lifted their coverings and exposed even their ankles.

I couldn't imagine what the sight of an ankle would do to poor Jamal. Surely he would have to pull to the side of the road to regain his composure. "If a woman is out and passes by her husband, will she ignore him or greet him?" I asked.

"No, never, madam, will the woman not greet her husband and offer him respect. It would be as she wants." Jamal was sure this was true.

But I wondered, would she take that moment of passing to claim the one freedom given by cover of the burqa—her anonymity?

My interactions with the Afghan women were sparse and stunted by language barriers. The few women with whom I was able to speak—some who worked in the embassy and some working with NGO partners—represented the more educated and most free. They said that identifying themselves in public depended on who they met but also on their mood.

The women were shy about talking candidly to a Western woman; building relationships and trust took time in this culture. When I offered my thoughts, they were usually received politely or with astonishment. For example, both the women and men had a hard time understanding how I could work so far from family and especially my husband.

One day, Mirian, a local hire in our office, asked me, "How did you convince your husband to let you come here to work?"

Given my husband's health and the struggle to decide to return to Afghanistan, this question was a bit sensitive and took me by surprise. I thought about it a moment and replied, "While I try to be considerate of my husband, he does not make those kinds of decisions for me."

Somewhat aghast, Miriam said, "I cannot imagine making such a decision. My husband is modern, but he would never let me travel alone and live for months in a strange land. I don't think my father-in-law would allow it either, nor my father or brother."

So many men controlling this woman's life, was my immediate thought. Looking at her earnest curiosity about me, I realized how different we were, almost down to our DNA level. I asked, "But you are allowed to work at the embassy. Does your family approve of this? Is this something new in your family?"

"My mother-in-law worked for a short time before the Taliban took over, so she was supportive of me," she answered. "She convinced my husband to allow me to work. When I interviewed, my husband came along with me and asked many questions about my job, who I would work with, where I would sit, and so on. This is normal here, and he was convinced that I would be okay." Smiling, she went on, "And I think the thought of the extra money helped too."

It is unfathomable to me for women to be completely dominated by the males in society. Certainly the most control is in the immediate family, but even strangers might object to some public behavior. The passivity bred into these women through their society, culture, and religion was so deep that even the most educated women among them often did not recognize it in themselves. They could express a desire for more freedom but seemed to have a very limited vision of what that freedom might be.

To the women, as well as the men, Western women were practically a third gender.

Chapter 12

The Camel and the Tunnel

Neither the camel nor its owner really cared about me. Their job was to signal that the tunnel was clear of stuck cars, trucks, or animals and ready for new travelers from the opposite direction—in my case, coming up from the south to pass through. It mattered little how I felt about entering this deep, dark hole that was one of the highest tunnels in the world, plunging through and piercing the towering mountain range of the Hindu Kush. *Hindu Kush* translates to the "unforgiving mountains" or "killer mountains"—not a reassuring thought as I prepared to enter the bombed-out Salang Tunnel.

The Salang Tunnel was considered an engineering wonder when the Soviet Union constructed it in 1964 after ten long years of planning. It is located in the Hindu Kush Mountains of northern Afghanistan at an elevation of 11,154 feet. At the time, it was the highest elevation tunnel in the world. The two-kilometer (approximately one and a half miles) tunnel was the only all-weather route from Kabul traveling directly north to the northern provinces of Afghanistan. It allowed travelers to avoid a much longer, more circuitous route to the east through Bamiyan and central Afghanistan. That route added approximately 186 miles and eighteen hours of tortuous, body-slamming, and vehicle-punishing travel to each trip in order to reach the cities north of the tunnel—rather like going around your elbow to get to your ear. Also, this longer route was precarious and fraught with danger, featuring poorly constructed roads and sparsely populated villages.

And so, the use of the Salang Tunnel was a popular route. To my utter amazement, when I checked on the estimated use, I learned that hundreds of vehicles a day passed through the tunnel. Seeing the barren and isolated mountain ranges, I marveled that there were even a hundred functioning vehicles anywhere in the entire region, let alone that traveled the difficult route daily. I was to learn the longer I stayed in Afghanistan that things are rarely what they seem. One expects one thing and finds another. I would enter a village expecting to find all uneducated people and find an educated philosopher. I would enter a bombed-out compound and find a beautiful rose garden within its walls. I would consider an area to be remote and unpopulated and instead find thousands of people living in little villages hidden in nooks and crannies within the mountains. Similarly, the lives of the people often remain hidden to the outsider much like those hundreds of vehicles a day. I quickly learned that unless I dug deep and sought out the truth, it would evade me.

In the late 1990s, when the fighting between the Taliban and the northern *mujahideen* was raging, General Ahmad Shah Massoud had been forced to bomb and cripple the tunnel. Massoud, who rose to be the charismatic leader of the Northern Alliance resistance army, had agonized over destroying this vital artery that provided access for much of his food and supplies. Hence, he decided to only cripple the tunnel, not completely destroy it. This temporary cessation of access would protect his area of control from a Taliban incursion from the south, at least via this route. Massoud's destruction was very effective. He managed to destroy the ventilation system, the water drainage system, and the electrical system inside of the tunnel. He also blew up its south entrance, narrowing the internal passageway and thus preventing military equipment from passing through. These essential elements of tunnel safety soon became critical to our activities and the humanitarian flow of people and supplies. The damage to the tunnel, resulting in critical safety concerns, limitation of vehicle movement, and provision of humanitarian supplies, was the reason behind my visit to the tunnel that day. Early on after America had defeated the Taliban and weakened its control of Afghanistan, the Afghan refugees in Pakistan started to return home. Many of them were trying to get home to the north and so needed this tunnel to be safe and open for them

Shortly after I arrived at the US embassy in February of 2002, I began getting reports of large numbers of local civilians and returning refugees being trapped inside the tunnel and dying from either exposure or asphyxiation. The numbers were rising monthly as more and more local people began to move commercial supplies and personal goods back to the northern regions of Afghanistan following on the heels of the early successes of the combined US Special Forces and Northern Alliance forces. The liberation of the region and defeat of the Taliban after the 9/11 attack seemed assured. Neither the US embassy nor the US military wanted to see these civilian deaths occur or become headlines around the world. So the Office of US Foreign Disaster Assistance (OFDA) was asked to intervene, if possible, with a program to improve the safety of travel for those civilians using the tunnel. It was my job to review proposals from the NGOs, inspect the tunnel, and work with the local elders to formulate a plan to do that. This was a very unusual intervention for our office to take up. And, let's be clear here, I don't know anything about tunnels, especially those through mountains in Afghanistan. But I had a very talented group of engineers working with a French NGO to advise me and propose a plan to my team for funding consideration. They traveled with me, and that is how and why I came to be standing outside that massive, jagged hole in a mountain range one cold day in February 2002 in a foreign land with a camel and a mountain village man who had nothing to say to me.

Massoud's tactical success in crippling the tunnel had become my personal, professional, and humanitarian nightmare.

I waited at the southern entrance of the tunnel. Already my day had been full of emotional highs and lows starting from seven that morning. I set off from Kabul with four staff members from the French NGO. The embassy wanted me to take along a small contingent of US military personnel consisting of engineers and force protection staff for safety as well, and I wanted a couple of members of my humanitarian team from the embassy to come along. The trip route would cover more than fifty-three miles over some of the most treacherous roads in the world. Our five-vehicle caravan carried about twenty people who would inspect the famous Salang Tunnel.

The journey took four hours along narrow, gut-wrenching roads that clung precariously to the sides of steep mountains. Periodically we drove through avalanche shelters that had been constructed to catch the sliding snow and ice coming off the near-vertical hillsides. The shelters were constructed in the shadowed areas of the jagged, white-tipped mountains with the purpose of protecting the passing vehicles below on the narrow roads. It was like carefully driving through a carport that resembled a wooden shack. We passed through with nothing much for protection except our prayers, relying on the years of previous service of these structures to assure ourselves of the sturdiness of each overhang. We crossed under one rickety avalanche shelter after another. Negotiating these overhangs and sharp curves along the route took maximum concentration of the drivers. We all tried to keep the talking to a minimum as we wanted no distractions. Plus, we were all both fascinated with the austere surroundings and full of fear at how dangerous each curve was.

Freezing cold silver rivers ran down from the mountainsides and wove around us as we drove, necessitating numerous one-lane wooden bridges. Again, in true Afghan style, beauty and beast met. When we dared to look, we saw magnificent mountain vistas, pristine snow-covered valleys, and villages untouched by time. As I looked around, I wondered, *Am I in a place on earth in the twenty-first century, or have I been transported to some unknown time of yesteryear?* It is not possible to overstate the differences in culture and life between America and the far rural villages of Afghanistan. There was life all around but hidden from strangers' eyes. I saw nothing moving to indicate the magnitude of life that was sustained in the mountains. Had it been later, in spring or summer, I might have seen men working in the fields, but in this frozen landscape, all was quiet—or so it seemed. Women were trapped inside small stone huts that I occasionally could see, sorting out food, preparing meals, washing clothes, keeping the home fires going and giving birth to new generations of Afghans. These women survive on little more than their determination and their inner belief that this is the only way of life—Allah's will.

On the route, we passed a place where a bridge had collapsed the week before, tumbling a bus into one of those rushing icy mountain rivers below. The passengers' bodies had been removed, but the bus remained. The metal was just beginning to rust, a rust I knew would spread like a ravaging cancer until the bus was no longer recognizable. I imagined the travelers' last moments of safety as they approached the bridge, and then it began to creak, shake, give, and collapse, plunging them fifty feet below into the roaring river. I hoped that if such a thing were to happen to me, I would die instantly rather than suffer long hours in this cold, remote place. I was learning that there was never any lack of fuel for the imagination here. The trick was to not let it stop me from trudging onward during my time in Afghanistan.

We finally arrived at the tunnel. A tired, dirty camel and its human master both stared at me. Just like I had never seen such roadside workers before, I knew that the camel and the man had never seen a Western woman before.

I dreaded going forward into the tunnel. Actually, I hated it. To avoid the inevitable, I stalled; I smiled and said, "*Salam Alakum*" to the small, weathered man. He wore a rather grimy, tattered blue blazer over a brown sweater and his earth-toned shalwar kameez, the traditional Afghan dress of loose trousers and long tunic-like shirt. On top of his head was a brown turban that matched his suntanned, wrinkled skin. He had a long scraggly beard in conformity with the stricter Islamic sects. The rest of his clothes, including a small blanket slung over the left shoulder, were in understated, neutral tones that made him blend in with his environment.

He gazed back at me but said nothing. Could my boldness in speaking first have angered him? I was always second-guessing my actions for politeness and appropriateness in this new culture. Maybe he was a believer in an Islamic practice of not exchanging "*Salam Alakum*" with infidels? I was certainly not local and therefore most probably an infidel.

I would eventually get used to the stares and unresponsiveness of Afghan men, but at that moment it was still new to me. Some men were shy, but most simply didn't know what to do with me. Their women were the silent bearers of their children and the keepers of their homes. They certainly would never be so bold as to initiate talk with a strange man.

I could handle a silent Afghan, but the tunnel I wasn't so sure about. It was a crumbling black hole that cut into the belly of the mountain. Looking more like a cave than a man-made tunnel, its roof was the string of rocky, barren mountains high above us. I took a few long breaths, feeling overwhelmed at having to enter it. I turned to my companions for the day and said, "I don't think I can go in." I could feel my breaths coming in short, rapid bursts. I am extremely claustrophobic. I felt like I was about to enter a tomb. "Most Americans can't even locate this place on a map. What if something happens?" I asked.

I turned to my Afghan colleague, Abdulaman, a rugged middle-aged man hired to accompany me on the journey. "Are we crazy to be going in?" I said.

"The way has been cleared for you," he said in a calm voice. "You cannot refuse to go through the tunnel. I am told that a meeting has been arranged on the northern side for you. They will be waiting for 'the visiting dignitary'—you." That was all he said. As usual, all the men that I was to meet in Afghanistan were men of few words, even the interpreters, whose job it was to talk.

Our goal for the trip and the meeting was to figure out a plan to stop the ever-increasing death toll resulting from trapped vehicles within the tunnel. Whatever plan that was decided on had to be acceptable to the local population. Afghan refugees, mostly from Pakistan on this side of the country, were desperate to travel home. Humanitarian supplies were needed, and the tunnel needed to be safe for our teams to travel through. This was the only connecting road that remained open throughout the winter. All around me felt peaceful, but the silence was deceiving. The fight for control of the north was not completed, and pockets of Taliban or Northern Alliance troops were hidden in the hills. I had no idea who might be watching us through binoculars.

The tunnel had been poorly maintained even when it was still new, and the long, brutal war; punishing climate; and high usage had taken a further toll on its overall condition. The strategic bombing by the Northern Alliance forces was the final insult to this rather primitive passageway. I was struck by how isolated we were should some mishap occur. It was like being on a mountainous moon landscape.

I began to understand why the tunnel had trapped and killed so many people. Not one village was within sight of it, and no emergency service vehicles or staff were nearby to provide assistance.

By eleven fifteen, the camel had come and gone and I had to enter the tunnel to inspect it. This was not a time to wimp out. I felt the weight of representing Westerners and the women of the world (okay, a bit dramatic, but there were all these men waiting for me to get started). I thought of the repressed women in Afghanistan who were told daily that they could do nothing—that they *were* nothing. That they needed a man to survive.

With those incentives pushing me onward, I gritted my teeth and got into my vehicle.

My four-by-four Jeep, driven by the intrepid Abdulaman, bumped and twisted over blasted rocks and debris that straddled the approach to the narrowed tunnel entrance. As we pushed onward, deeper into the tunnel, I saw how so many large trucks got stuck, sliding on the icy route and becoming wedged in the narrow passageway. The reports were of someone getting stuck almost every day. One blocked truck would make for a nightmarish traffic jam; there was no way to get two-lane traffic through this narrow tunnel. I'd been told that when that happened, travelers were sometimes stranded for days at a time.

As we traveled deeper inside, I smelled the foul air and remembered that the ventilation system had been destroyed. My mind began to rush, imagining all kinds of calamities. Without lights, ventilation, or drainage, I feared getting stuck in this icy cave. It smelled damp and cold. Condensation collected on the cold walls and froze along the sides, creating a duct of ice and icicles that further narrowed the tunnel and turned it into a wet, slippery, frosty tube. I felt the Jeep slipping and sliding from side to side. No sun had ever touched the inside of this cold passageway. Even the best, bravest, and most stalwart of Afghan drivers were at high risk of becoming the driver of the next wedged truck. I wondered if that would be us.

Our procession of vehicles made slow progress. Each car stayed a good distance behind the one in front just in case there was an accident. With the icy, uneven conditions, we could not stop quickly.

In spite of having a group with me, my mind ran away with possibilities. How desperate would I become if we were stranded here? Would we keep the engines running for warmth? I could imagine myself stranded, entombed, freezing, and trying to stay warm while asphyxiating myself on carbon monoxide fumes. I couldn't stop my imagination from running wild. Could we walk out of the tunnel? It might be possible if ours was either the first or the last cars entering the tunnel, but once we were in the middle, it felt like it would be impossible; we'd be faced with a harrowing mile-long hike in the cold and dark, with precarious footing on the icy ground. And all the while, the tunnel would be full of vehicles with engines spewing deadly fumes.

Even though there were about twenty of us, I still felt very frightened and measured the risks as if I were alone. Could I walk out? I just didn't know.

With the help of the Jeep's headlights, I could see the damage inside the tunnel. The walls of cracked ice looked ready to collapse. Needing reassurance, I peppered my guide with questions: "What is the width here? What is creating all the ice? How does it get into the middle of the tunnel?"

"The tunnel has many leaks that allow water to enter from the heavy mountains overhead," he answered. (That was a piece of information I didn't need pointed out to me!) "The snow melt-off creates many underground streams that find their way into the tunnel," Abdulaman's deep voice echoed off the icy walls. "It is why repairing the drainage system is so important."

I did not feel reassured.

I couldn't see the exit. There was no sign of daylight. Just then I realized that our hand radios didn't work inside the tunnel. I hadn't considered that before entering. I could not remember the last time I had felt so frightened. I was beginning to feel like I was buried in an icy, cold tomb.

"Are you sure that no vehicle will enter from the north?" I asked, yet again.

"Madam, please do not worry. We have taken care of everything," said Abdulaman with the patience of someone long practiced in reassuring women. Was I failing on the "I am woman, I am strong" test?

"But what is the plan when we get to the north side? I want us to keep on schedule so it's not dark when we head back through the tunnel." I'm afraid I might have whined a bit. *Wait a minute*, I thought, *it's always dark in the tunnel.* "I mean, we can't travel the mountain roads after dark," I corrected myself.

"I will watch the time. I do not want to drive the mountain roads in the dark either," assured Abdulaman.

Residual carbon monoxide fumes hung thick in the air. The trick was to not spend too much time in the tunnel, I thought, as we inched our way slowly onward. The ice accumulation sparkled in the headlights of our cars. I watched as the vehicle ahead of us slipped from side to side. Our jeep did the same. We were travelling at perhaps two to five miles per hour. Maybe it would have been better to measure our progress in feet. We stopped often to inspect a spot of particular decay within the tunnel. It made for a long two kilometers.

Finally, I saw light—or was I hallucinating? Was that a symptom of carbon monoxide poisoning? I checked with Abdulaman. "Do you see the light?" I asked. Yes, it was true, we really were nearing the exit on the northern side. I felt such relief and decided not to think about the return trip at that moment.

We exited the tunnel and burst into the brightness found only on mountaintops. The sun hurt my eyes, and the relief made me feel light-headed. Or was that the clear, fresh mountain air? I almost started laughing. It was hard to regain my composure and ready myself for the next event of the day—our meeting with the Afghan mountain elders who were the leaders in the surrounding villages. I could only hope that they would accept meeting with a woman after all I'd gone through to get to them.

A group of about fifteen elders were waiting for us as we exited.

"Where did they come from? I wondered how long they had to travel to get here. I don't see any villages or towns around," I said.

"Being seen is not safe," Abdulaman explained. "There are many villages in these mountains, but they are located in places so as not to be seen. They use the earth and its colors for their homes. Hiding in plain site is a specialty of the Afghan villages and its people." I knew of this trick, hiding and blending in so as to not be noticed. Survival during decades of war had taught them the lesson of invisibility, as it had taught me in my childhood. It made for a common thread between the Afghan people and me.

We followed the waiting tribal leaders to the meeting site, a room in a dilapidated earth-toned building just north of the tunnel's exit. The floor was made of packed dirt, and what little light there was inside came from small, dirty windows and three smoky kerosene lanterns. Again we had the odor of fumes and the semidarkness to adjust to. I heard the shifting of bodies before I could see anyone. In this shadowed room, there arose a sweet, pungent smell. I wondered if there were animals in the room. Animals in proximity to human living spaces is not unusual in rural farming communities in these isolated primitive villages.

Slowly, my eyes began to adjust to the nearly dark room. Still, it was hard to distinguish one *mujahideen* from another. Brown, gray, and tan surrounded me: in the walls, ceiling, floor, and men. They all blurred together. The council of elders inside this simple meeting room were from the many villages hidden in the mountains of the Hindu Kush.

The whiff of horse, camel, and sheep carried on the men's clothing explained my sense of animals nearby. Their loose, flowing trousers tied at the waist did not confine the odors of bodily excretions, while their long, untucked shirts held the smell of unwashed torsos.

As I took in these familiar but misplaced scents, I thought, *they must smell me, too.* I wore perfume every day—as a comfort and conciliation to my rough living conditions and in deference to my puritanical, sanitized American upbringing. Did my new smell excite them? Repulse them? Offend them? Confuse them? And could they smell the remnants of my fear from the tunnel?

As I retreated toward a wall, no one greeted me or, heaven forbid, touched me. There was the hum of chatter in their unknown dialect, a buzz of questions. "They ask, why you are here and what are they to do with you?" Abdulaman whispered to me. "They did not expect to meet with a woman." For a few moments, confusion reigned until Abdulaman explained my presence. Still there seemed to be some question of what they should to do with me. I knew this was best left to the locals to decide along with Abdulaman. In the midst of all this, the military escorts were outside surveying the situation. What a juxtaposition—a woman inside negotiating, and men outside doing their thing. It would have been comical if the day hadn't already been full of dangerous travel and I wasn't heading into some serious discussions.

Shifting my eyes downward, I noticed the blanket on the dirt floor over which was an abundance of local food. A feast of traditional Afghan fare was being offered. As I began to decipher the various aromas wafting up from the floor, I could smell grilled lamb. There was also rice with side dishes of nuts, dried fruits, and water or Cokes. I smiled. This universal drink seemed to be ubiquitous. It did not always taste the same and might be served warm, but Coke was often served. It was a favorite for Afghans who do not drink alcohol. Not trusting the sanitation of the water, warm Coke was my drink of choice that day.

I was nervously aware of the time passing. I didn't want to look like I was in a hurry for fear of insulting my hosts, but I was worried about the long trip home. The men continued to be unsure about what to do with me and were spending some considerable time discussing issues without including me. I was a new wrinkle in their plans for the day.

I asked my guide, "Why are they all staring at me? Do they understand that I am the person they must discuss the tunnel management with?"

He responded simply, "You are a woman."

He seemed to think that was all the explanation needed.

It was obvious that, aside from meeting with the men, sitting for a meal with them was also a major deviation from tradition. Where was I to sit? We all had to sit on the floor. It was just a matter of who sat where and next to whom. We would eat off the well-used cloth on the floor. Being the only woman in a room full of fierce-looking and definitely confused—maybe even angry—Afghan men was a problem.

So I just dropped to the floor and let them work out where they would sit. In the end, they all sat on the other side of the cloth across from me. I felt a little lonely on my side of the blanket. Some of the NGO staff and my translator came to my side. Having a nonrelative man sit next to me was no small break in custom, and it took courage.

The worse, though, was yet to come. The local elders *had* to talk with me; I was the team leader. I was in charge. I had the money. The Afghan men certainly would have been much more at home talking to the drivers or the local employees, but alas, it was me or no one.

Everyone dug into the meal with the gusto of hungry, hard-working men.

"Please tell me how the tunnel is functioning," I asked as the bread was passed.

Pause. Total silence. Was it taboo to talk while eating or just for me, as a woman, to open up the conversation?

"Is the death toll coming down from the previous month?"

Again, no one answered.

I finally looked to Abdulaman. "How is your food?"

"Oh, very fine," he said with obvious relief. "The elders will speak about the conditions once they have eaten. Be patient."

And so, gently chastised by my driver/translator, I settled into eating my food.

Serving the men would have been a more acceptable role for me I thought. That would be a more in line with their traditions, but even that would not happen with nonrelated men in the room. It was awkward.

Gradually, my hosts talked to Abdulaman, relaying information about the existing situation and the strengths and weaknesses of the proposed program that had been discussed with them previously by the NGO hoping to execute the program. There was discussion about the challenges of keeping the tunnel open every day and about keeping the transiting cars and trucks safe. Abdulaman told the men that I was there to assess possibilities of funding for many of the needs and to monitor the efficiency of the changes that would be made in the management of the tunnel. There was a suggestion to institute alternating days for north and south traffic to prevent head-on traffic jams inside, an important change that would need to be conveyed to all in the surrounding area. It was assumed that it would not take long for word of this shift to reach all who routinely traveled the route. Also, the surrounding villages would need to assume some responsibility of responding to emergencies.

"It would be wonderful to have a small backhoe or tractor stationed here to pull out the stuck vehicles," one of the hosts commented.

"It would be great, but we don't have one. And who would maintain it? And where would we park it when it's not in use?" I said. "Could the village bring one up here for the days the tunnel is open and we could pay rent to use it?"

The men looked at me like I was truly from another planet, clearly wondering how I had come up with that idea—any idea, for that matter.

Meanwhile, in the midst of discussion and the tension, I was trying to remember not to eat with my left hand. This was the hand traditionally reserved for cleaning one's bottom after toileting and thus considered unclean. There were a plethora of rules and customs that I had the opportunity to break. I tried to focus on breaking *only* those necessary for me to get business done, but not so many as to create a chasm between us. I had business to conclude that day.

There was silence for a few minutes before one of the local men said, "Why don't I see if I can get a local vehicle to be available for rent?"

Now really, where did he get that idea? Oh, I was going to love working with Afghan men.

I nodded and told my translator, "That is such a good idea. Let's have them work on it, and we will make sure that there are funds for the NGO team to pay local help as needed. But they must come when called and needed, not just when they want to come. Is that understood?"

More discussion ensued among the men.

Finally, the leader replied, "Oh, yes, all is understood and agreed on."

There was more discussion, but I was constantly aware of the passing time. I explained to my translator that I had a curfew and had to be back in the embassy by dark. He explained this to the men around me.

Finally, something made sense to them: I was a woman, so of course I had a curfew. Meanwhile I was thinking, *I'm in an alternate universe. How did I get here?*

Chapter 13

Living with the US Marines

"Good morning, sunshine!" The fresh-faced marine guarding the front door to the American embassy greeted each morning as I walked up the steps to the door to start my day.

Guarding the embassy's front door deep inside of the compound during the early days of the Afghanistan invasion was long, boring duty. The Taliban were on the run. Kabul was in chaos, and America's partners, the Northern Alliance troops, were busy fighting the good fight in the mountains and collaborating with the US forces on the ground. NATO was setting up control of Kabul. The marines at the embassy were for safety and security, but luckily they saw little action. This marine guarding the front door had arrived at Bagram Air Force Base in the middle of the night and would leave in the middle of night. He would never see downtown Kabul during his mission. He would never leave the embassy compound. In these early days, the tours of duty were for three months.

He was young enough to be my son. He was lonely and bored and had little understanding of this magnificent land where he found himself guarding a door that few ever entered. He knew little or nothing of its long history. I was one of the highlights of his morning as I walked up smiling and happy for work. "Good morning, sunshine," and "Good morning, Corporal" had become our ritual greeting.

The marines like being seen as masters of their universe, protectors of the weak, and avengers of the injured. I, however, saw many of them as sweet, young, healthy, committed boys from America, although they would not have taken that as a compliment. But to me, many were just that.

Some were more hardened, but most had never seen combat in those early days of 2002 and still carried a romantic image of their role in "saving" America. I was grateful for and awed by them. They were committed and willing to die for me. It was the most humbling relationship of my life. I fervently hoped it never came to the test, but I trusted these young marines, who were so worthy of my respect and admiration. They were the best of the best.

The corporal from Kentucky opened the broken front door of the embassy for me, and my day began. I entered a world that few people experience. The lobby of the embassy was a cacophony of sounds and sights. There, on-duty and off-duty marines would hang around; they slept, ate, trained, and relaxed in the one building of the embassy. While in Afghanistan, it became their whole world. There was nowhere else for them to go.

The break room was to the right of the main entrance and often vibrated with cussing, shooting, and shouting from violent, B-list DVDs from America. The marines drank coffee or sodas and generally acted like eighteen- to twenty-year-olds would in any place in America. They *were* America here in this foreign land, from every state and every stratum of society. They were here to protect the embassy, but when off duty, they goofed off like like-minded youths in the States. I was always astonished that they wanted to watch those violent movies, but it seemed to keep them up, ready for anything. This was not date night at the movies with a pretty girl watching a romantic chick flick. This *was* Afghanistan and they *were always on duty*, even when off shift.

I passed through the lobby, hearing music and DVDs blaring, raucous laughter, and rough language in the break room. I only entered that room once—with another marine since this was the bastion of the boys. I knew they were lounging around in half-dress, telling crude jokes, and generally posturing as tough men worthy of the weapons lying at their feet.

This was an embassy, not a marines' barracks. But was it? It was also their barracks, and they were essential to our survival.

Often during meetings with high-level dignitaries from other embassies or government offices, I had to go out into the halls and reprimand them for their noise. One day, I was holding an important meeting with a representative of the World Bank in the upstairs foyer area in the open, as we had no private meeting rooms. We were sitting on a hastily found, dilapidated sofa and some chairs, discussing what the World Bank was planning to bring as support and programs to Afghanistan in the following year.

"Hey, what the fuck? Did you see that?" sounded out from below. "God damn, what the fuck were they doing?"

This was followed by laughter and more expletives. I was mortified. I excused myself and hurried downstairs to find a group of young marines laughing as they exited the break room. They looked much like high school seniors exiting the boys' locker room, heckling and jostling one another. I called out to get their attention. It took a minute before one of them noticed me yelling at them. They elbowed one another, and gradually the noise and laughter stopped.

About ten pair of eyes turned to me.

"Look, guys, this is a US embassy," I scolded them. "You cannot carry on like this in the lobby, and you most certainly cannot use such rough language in the public places. I am trying to have a high-level meeting upstairs, and we can hear you."

These were the boys who would die for me.

I felt awful calling them on the carpet, but the situation had to be dealt with immediately. I knew I was right to call for order in the open lobby of the embassy, but somehow, I hated to stop the spontaneous fun of these kids turned marines.

But, true to form, they became the men they had been trained to be: they stood there quietly and apologized.

"What's it like out there?" the marine guard asked me, meaning Kabul, when I returned to the embassy one day. He was nearing the end of his three-month assignment. He may as well have been protecting a ruined government building in downtown Washington, Houston, or New York City.

I tried to describe my day for him. "I met at the presidential palace with some of the interim government appointees. It is a beautiful, large spread of grand, old, softly colored brick buildings on grounds that must become gardens of some beauty in the summer. The roads are crowded with military vehicles from NATO, US military carriers, and International Security Assistance Forces (ISAF) vehicles," I told him. "The people walking around are mostly men in tan or gray clothes, but sprinkled among them is the hesitant shuffling of blue burqas."

"Why do the women still wear the coverings?" he asked, unfamiliar with the word *burqa*.

"They are fearful of what will happen when you and I leave. If the new government does not take hold, if it is not secured with military might to shore it up, they will be punished when reported for being without cover during this time. They will be beaten at best, and possibly killed," I told him. "So they will wait a while. They cannot trust in this new freedom enough to uncover."

Predictably, in his belief in his power to overturn wrong and protect the weak, he said, "But we are here, and the old Taliban ways are over."

I think he wanted the burqas to be gone as a sign of America's success.

It was so much more complicated, but none of us knew that yet.

Anyone who has lived in a house full of randy, high-functioning, fueled-up teenage boys can imagine the adrenaline rush of all these young men being together on lockdown in the embassy. Testosterone was overflowing, and it was paired with weapons and commanders and training and physical fitness on a daily basis to burn off some of the energy. The energy rubbed off on everyone until it burned itself out.

After a few months, there would be billiards and parties at night on the compound. But in the beginning, we were just there with maps on the walls, weapons on the floor, laptops in hand, and the hope of creating a new Afghanistan, free for all and safe for America.

The crew from *Good Morning America* arrived in Afghanistan. It was Mother's Day, 2002, and they knew many of us would like to greet our mothers on this special day. A filming and photo shoot were arranged for early in the morning, which was nine and a half hours ahead of New York time. We all sat on the embassy's front steps and shouted, on cue, "Good morning, America, from Afghanistan!" in hopes that it would be aired later that same day in America. Some of the staff were shy about being in the front row, and some did not want to be in the photo. But most of the civilians decided it would be fun, and so we prepared for our TV debut. We practiced saying, "Good morning, America" in unison. We wanted to be good, and we wanted our families to see us looking good. It was a warm May morning with the ever-present sun of Southeast Asia shining down on us. We had polished up as best we could, anticipating the moment when our families would see us, healthy and happy, sitting in this far-away land. Each of us had our own thoughts of what Mother's Day meant to us. For me as a daughter, mother, and new grandmother, I felt my aloneness. I thought of what I might have been doing were I at home. I would have had a shouting match with my mother in Florida— not because of a disagreement, but because she was so hard of hearing. Each call necessitated shouting. "I love you!" sounded like a threat or challenge. When she was done talking, she would say goodbye and just hang up, for all the world like I was done, too. I might have gone to North Carolina to visit my daughter, Rachel, the closest to us in Washington; her husband, David; and their beautiful little baby girl, Kate, born just nine days before the 9/11 attacks. I would have talked with my two sons, Eric in Connecticut with his wife, Stephani, and sweet little Alexandra, just one and half years old, and then with Jason, my World Trade Center survivor living in New Jersey. Mother's Day cards would have been exchanged with meaningful messages reminding each of us of the blessings of mothers. The days of my getting little-kid gifts made in art class in school or burnt toast and cereal in bed were long gone. But this was a first for me, being on the steps of the embassy in Kabul yelling "Good morning, America!" into cameras with colleagues all around. I decided to stand near the top step and let the more enthusiastic younger staff get the front rows. One of my younger colleagues made me smile with his homemade sign saying, "I love U!" for a wife back home. We all carried such heavy loads being in Afghanistan as we did our part to change the course of history. At least being on GMA was a bit of a lark in the otherwise dismal and serious business we were about.

It went off without a hitch, but I never did find out if it was used or not. We all asked our families, "Did you see me?" No one that I knew had. We moved so quickly on to the next thing that I don't remember if anyone else reported back on a family response—rather a let-down given the level of momentary excitement we had.

The first Fourth of July in Afghanistan marked a major milestone for the United States. A party was planned. It was to be the first official event at the newly reopened American embassy in Kabul and the event of the season on the grounds of the grand old dame of a building. The flower gardens had been brought back to life, the lawns were green, and the campers (including my home) were moved to the back of the embassy. It was in tip-top shape—for the shape it was in.

It was decided at the embassy that it was safe enough for us to celebrate our national holiday with an open reception on the grounds for approximately one hundred of Kabul's finest. The invitations were delivered by hand to colleagues and Afghan citizens alike. They were the hottest tickets in Kabul. Given the recent history between our two countries, this special invitation seemed to symbolize a turning point. Every detail was attended to—special foods in accordance with the Muslim faith needed to be served. Clearly, no pork products or beer or alcohol were served. There were also no baked beans; we just couldn't find any. And we did not have hot dogs or buns. But other than that, it was an American picnic. The food consisted of rolled meat patties, sliced fruits, candies, and little cakes. Juice was served, and the food was prepared ahead of time and set out under tents on long banquet tables. Party attendees could informally help themselves to the variety of foods and fruit drinks being offered. We had the obligatory speeches by the American ambassador, the leading Afghan government representatives, and UN dignitaries. Then, in a ceremony around our flag, the marines who were not working security paraded in in style. A color guard presented the flag, and it was raised. Someone had found a trumpet to play the American national anthem as well as a marine who could apparently play.

The crowd stood at attention, and the music began. Ooh, was that a bad note? Another, and then another? It became obvious that either it was a bad trumpet or the marine who had been recruited for the job could not actually play. Nevertheless, we all stood at attention as though the entire

US Marine Corps band was playing a beautiful rendition of our national anthem. We were full of pride, if a bit chagrined. And we were really in pain for the poor trumpeter, who stood bravely and played the entire song.

Jobs for the event had been assigned to each of the embassy staff. I was to be a greeter, which meant that I would stand at the embassy gate so that when guests, especially Afghan dignitaries, were cleared to enter, I could greet them and escort them the hundred feet or so to the front grounds of the embassy. I would make sure to introduce them to someone with whom they could visit and feel comfortable at the festivities. I tried to present each new guest to the ambassador and get a cool drink for him or her. I would then return to the front gate and greet my next assignee.

I chose my dress carefully for that day to be cheery and summery but in line with Afghan culture. It was a green and yellow flowered dress with elbow-length sleeves and an acceptable ankle length for a modest Western woman in this conservative culture. A slight concession to my Western roots were slits up both sides to just about my knees. When I tried it on in the store and walked in it, it seemed fine. But even the best thought-out plans can and usually did go awry in Afghanistan. The Fourth of July turned out to be sunny and warm but quite windy, as can happen in Kabul. Much to my chagrin, the wind took those flaps formed by the side slits and whipped them up about my legs. I was mortified as I tried to hold them down while escorting the guests. I felt rather foolish clutching at my flying skirt. I took a lot of kidding from the marines who, as healthy men, enjoyed the flash of female leg. It was nothing by our American standards but quite risqué for the Afghans. I remembered what Jamal, my driver, had said in my first weeks in Afghanistan about the thrill of a windy day.

Outside our embassy gates, I would have been beaten for such a display of flesh. I lived with this knowledge for my fellow women each day.

The security staff and undercover marines milled around the grounds throughout the party, keeping a close eye on everyone. There is an art to giving a party and keeping security tight but unobtrusive.

In spite of the work assignments and the wind, we all had a great time. The party brought together Afghans, other embassies' staff in Kabul, UN heads of offices, NGO country directors, and Americans working in Kabul. We all spent a delightful and safe afternoon milling around the front grounds under tents, shaded from the sun and making the standard small talk of all cocktail parties.

"Hi, Marcel! It's good to see you here in the city after our last trip to the north," I said, greeting a French colleague from the UN.

"This is quite a display of Americana you have going on today," he replied.

"Yes, it is a time-honored tradition for American embassies around the world to sponsor Fourth of July parties and quite a statement that we can even have an open one here in Kabul given the year's events. It's been a lot of work, and lots of safety precautions were taken while still trying to keep a relaxed, party atmosphere. How do you think we've done?"

"It's a great success, I think," Marcel responded. "I am having a wonderful time as are all the people I've visited with. The food is really good, if a bit unusual for an American Fourth of July party."

"Have as much as you like. We have plenty of food with little space for storage, so do help yourself," I said as I moved on to someone I saw standing alone. I was very aware that this was a working day for us staff, and as such, I needed to mix as much as possible.

I caught snatches of conversations as I moved around. Some discussed the traditions of Fourth of July parties in America with Afghan attendees trying to learn what American life was like. Some conversations were more serious, but these were limited given the lack of privacy. I heard plans being made for appointments in the coming days and questions about procedural matters. Many Afghans were huddled together in small groups talking in Pashtun. But on the whole, the conversations that I participated in or overheard were of the normal chatter for any party. The beauty of this party was that those clusters of people talking spoke in multiple languages and were arrayed in a variety of unique national dress. And yet, surprisingly, the low hum of voices was sprinkled with a good bit of laughter.

It was considered the social event of the summer of 2002, when turmoil often reigned and the war in Afghanistan was still being defined. It marked the summer of hopes and dreams for all of us. Celebrating the birth of our nation on the soil of Afghanistan was a prayer for that ancient and proud country—that it, too, might have a new birth in freedom and prosperity.

Connecting with home was challenging but always felt important, especially on holidays or birthdays. During these days back in Afghanistan, I tried to call home once a week or so. It was difficult to connect, but by this time the embassy had set up its communications system and we were allowed to make brief calls back home. The cell phone service in Kabul was still very poor, and the public phone system was both unreliable and unsafe to use.

My days were busy, and the weeks seemed to be flying by. Back home, I knew that Mike and the kids were still worried about me being in Afghanistan, but I had gotten in such a routine of working and living that I often forgot about the strain for loved ones back home. I was feeling more and more disconnected. I had this new life, living and working under unusual circumstances. I had established a solid routine, and days began to feel normal. When I gave myself time to think about my other life, it felt foreign. This is why it was so important for me to call home and stay engaged in what was my real life.

Mike was doing well. He had gone back to work and was eating healthily and exercising each day. He got good reports from his cardiologist and generally was feeling better than he had in years. I was feeling less and less guilty about being away. The kids were all moving on in their personal lives with new babies, homes, and jobs. Jason seemed to be bouncing back from the 9/11 attacks and was working again in New York. I knew that he still struggled occasionally from panic attacks, but they were less severe and less frequent. I tried to convey to each of them what my life was like, but it was difficult since nothing was relatable for them or normal for me. The experience of living with military personnel at an embassy in the emerging war zone of Afghanistan was hard to convey. It was also confusing for me to assimilate the changes in my life as it shifted so radically.

Chapter 14

Attacks on the American Embassy

Freedom would not come easily or quickly in Afghanistan. The embassy was always on full alert, and this reality hung over us daily. At times, I worked as though I was in Washington. I wrote reports. I discussed new programs with my staff. I got reports from them on their areas of specialty. We planned, devised new strategies, and coordinated with other donors— from friendly and not-so-friendly countries. I met with British, Russian, Iranian, Swiss, French, and Italian dignitaries in Kabul. We discussed the humanitarian needs of the civilians. I did not represent US diplomatic policy, and most certainly I did not represent the US military. I was around both groups and soaked up information from both, but I did not speak of any of it. I talked only of the women and children, the old and the dying in Kabul and around the country with whom we were not at war. I hoped to meet their basic human rights as best as possible within the limitations of my resources.

But many saw me as more than I was. All of us assigned in the embassy were aware of this as we worked within the scope of our jobs. My colleagues were professionals of the highest caliber. I learned from them, and as we learned together, we were always aware of the surroundings in which we did our jobs. When we forgot, the less-than-friendly Afghans reminded us. There were threats of attacks every week at the embassy—some were real, some apparently not.

On days when attacks happened in the form of missiles launched at the embassy, we would get a warning via the marines running around the building telling us that there were incoming missiles. At that point, we'd run to the basement of the main embassy building, which served as our bomb shelter. In fact, that happened so often that it became routine, or as routine as being under attack can be. The embassy had not been upgraded with external bomb shelters, which would later become a common sight around the grounds of the new embassy. In the beginning, the physical structures and technology were rather primitive. Our "bomb shelter" was what anyone might imagine a basement to be—full of boxes, old furniture (but very few chairs, since I always seemed to be sitting on the floor), old file cabinets, and high, dirty windows that let in some light. We were instructed to stay as far away from the windows as possible. The one concession to good planning were stacks of boxes with MREs and cases of fresh water. I was never sure if they were there in the event of a long stay in the shelter or just because that was the storage place for supplies. I soon learned that if I was to go to the basement, I should bring something to read. The long waits just sitting down there were either highly stressful events or just plain boring. When there was nothing I could do, I worried less than if I was responsible for something. I fell in the bored group. We all noticed that the more seasoned staff brought either work or magazines to read. On one of my first duck-and-covers, I saw a colleague with a coveted American women's magazine and envied her this diversion. We might be stuck in the basement twenty to forty minutes before a marine came downstairs to tell us that it was clear to return to our offices. That was a long time to just sit quietly and look at one another. From then on, I had some reading material ready on my desk to pick up as I ran out of the room. Time spent in the basement went much faster and was less stressful when reading a good novel or thumbing through a magazine. It was a little more difficult to bring work material, as that usually required our computers for revisions or ongoing work, or it was sensitive and could not leave our offices. On the whole, the basement time either gave us time to read or meet new staff who might be working in other sections of the embassy. Talking was usually hushed and stilted to allow for listening to radio transmissions and instructions.

Sometimes we heard the explosions, and sometimes we didn't. It depended on how close the bombs were and also on the caliber of weapons. I remember being very grateful for the marines who stood outside, ready to return fire if needed. Generally this was not the case since the missiles were shot from some distant location.

Ironically, after weeks of the attacks, we came to the conclusion that the safest place to be when the US embassy was being attacked was inside the embassy. Apparently the aiming devices were rather crude or the enemy were poor shots. The missiles struck a Japanese compound behind us, the Afghan Ministry of Public Health next to us, and the field across the street from us. The target—us—was not hit; it was just the near misses that struck those unfortunate enough to be located around us. But we still had to duck with each threat. I came to know the basement well or, when there was not time to get to the basement, the underside of my desk where I spent some twenty to thirty minutes during those attacks waiting for the all clear to be given. We never heard if there were casualties in the outside buildings but assumed so if there had been a direct hit. It seems odd that this piece of information was not the top of our concern. Our focus was on making it through our day. I suppose had there been casualties or structural damage, we would have heard about it.

Each day the work of upgrading security in and around the embassy continued. When I first arrived, there were no loudspeakers and no alarm systems. All warnings had to be passed by word of mouth. This was not so challenging in the daytime, when most of us who were on the compound were in the embassy building itself. But as the weather improved, I often held meetings at a picnic table outside. On those days, someone would have to run outside to convey the threat to everyone on the grounds. This was always unnerving to our guests, whom we had to bring along with us to the shelter area. They then became inadvertent captives during the attack. As soon as it was safe, they usually hurried off and, I'm sure, conveyed their adventure to their colleagues. They also usually became the colleagues least likely to agree to future meetings on our embassy grounds. This meant that I had to get clearance and permission to go to their locations to hold meetings. I didn't mind this as it broke up my day and got me out and about in the city. While it provided an opportunity to see more of Kabul, it was much less efficient timewise than holding back-to-back meetings within the embassy.

One day I was meeting with a Russian embassy emergency response professional when there was a security threat. "Excuse me, Mr. Keranovska, we need to run into the embassy basement to hide until an all clear is given. Please follow me," I said calmly. He looked rather shocked, and in his broken English he said, "I will leave now if you don't mind."

"Well, actually," I said, "you cannot leave as the gates won't open while we are under threat. The marines will not let you out."

"Do you mean I am a prisoner?"

"Oh, my God, no, but just for your safety, we need to get to cover immediately. Then after the all clear, you will be free to go," I quickly explained. But still he didn't like it.

We proceeded to the back entrance to the basement of the embassy and sat in uncomfortable chairs with everyone else while the American marines stayed outside to face whatever might be coming. Hopefully, it would be another miss.

It was. We were lucky.

Finally everyone was dismissed after about twenty-five minutes. Mr. Keranovska decided to stay and finish our meeting, but I am quite sure that he returned to the Russian embassy with tales of his adventure being held captive in our basement while the American embassy was under attack. And so another day passed for me.

At night, however, warnings involved a more interesting process. The marines still had to run around to notify everyone. Their most immediate concern was, of course, the ambassador and all the other marines. My most memorable nighttime security event happened in the spring of 2002, when there was a credible report of incoming missiles—maybe dirty (chemical) missiles. The on-duty marines immediately warned the off-duty marines, who jumped out of their bunks, roused everyone as assigned, and led them to the basement. This included everyone from the ambassador on down in rank. By this time, I was living in my small German camper brought in to get us out of the underground bunker. It was located on the side grounds of the main embassy building. I was awakened from a deep sleep by the sound of knocking on my door in the middle of the night. In a daze, I went to the door. There was no peephole, so I just opened it and stood in amazement. It appeared that Darth Vader had come to call. There stood a man in the dark in a mask and helmet.

"What's happening?" I asked, stunned.

"We are under attack, ma'am," said the marine. "Run to the basement."

I couldn't help pausing for a second to take in the scene. The marines were required to always don their essential gear—boots and personal protection equipment such as bulletproof vests, helmets, and gas masks in case of dirty bombs. And of course they had to carry their weapons. But apparently, nonessential clothing was *not* necessary in emergencies, as the marine at my door was wearing his essential gear but no trousers or shirt, just the briefs that he slept in. He spoke to me through his mask in a muffled voice yelling, "Incoming! Run to the basement!"

It took a second to register all this, but it was so worth the pause to fix the image. He was, after all, a fit, trim marine in essential gear only. We were both pumped up on adrenaline and in a hurry, but later I lamented the lack of a camera.

As the summer progressed, the marines continued to do their work. They improved communications with an alarm system that replaced the necessity of personal notifications for any danger. They also installed a protective perimeter of trip wires to detect anyone who might try to sneak onto the grounds. The surrounding wall was of little use, being only about three feet high, so the secondary wire barrier would give the alarm if the first was crossed.

These trip-wire alarms went off with some regularity day and night, keeping us all on our toes and ready to defend our ground if needed. The marines were always armed and ready to protect. The cat burglars who came to steal and forage in the night were always detected by the trip wires—that is, actual four-legged cats. We were at the mercy of the many cats of Kabul. While the marines had devised systems of protection from our mortal enemies for us, they were overwhelmed by the stray calico cats.

It became rather a joke around the embassy that we kept hiding from cats. Kabul is known for its many cats, many of which roam the streets at night. Eventually the marines rose to the situation and developed a new protective system that was neither so low to the ground nor so sensitive as to respond to the movement of cats.

Another adjustment to living in a war zone.

Author with camel at the Salang Tunnel on early spring visit, 2002

South entrance of the bombed-out Salang Tunnel in spring 2002

Author in burqa that is too short, with two colleagues from the embassy standing behind her camper. The grassy knoll to the right is the underground bunker; the stone wall covers the steps to go down under.

Author's camper, small one on the left, looking at the side of the old US embassy with a little round table for gathering outside behind it.

Author with Ambassador Finn and General Dostum leaving
the general's compound in Mazar-i-Sharif, April 2002

The Warlords

General Daud, the man in the
middle, the "Baby General"

General Ahmad Massoud,
the Lion of Panjshir

General Atta Mohammed Noor,
the man in the suit on the right

General Dostum, the
"Butcher of the North"

Our own American general,
General Dan K. McNeill

Author with the ambassador's protection team while
traveling in northern Afghanistan

The Blue Mosque in Mazar-i-Sharif, Afghanistan

Meeting on the presidential grounds in Kabul, Afghanistan,
with military planners for humanitarian programs >>

Author with "shopping consultants" on Chicken Street in downtown Kabul

Good Morning America photo shoot on the steps of the old embassy on Mother's Day, 2002. Our dear plumber is standing on the top step to the right in his coveralls. The author is the third persons to his left.

The look-alikes: Ambassador Chamberlain
on the left, author on the right

Chapter 15

A Day of Travel with the American Ambassador

When traveling anywhere in the world, an American ambassador's schedule is tightly planned, down to the minute. The time it takes to make a bathroom stop, take a drink of water, and make a call are all calculated into the day's events. And so the time of the American ambassador in Kabul was tightly controlled. We often joked that if his shoelace came untied, he would throw off the schedule when he bent to tie it. And in a country that was at war with many unregulated, out-of-uniform militias, security was at its tightest. Every detail along a route was controlled. Usually the host country participated in some portion of the security detail, but in the case of Afghanistan in the summer of 2002, there were no well-trained, reliable, or trusted Afghan police to provide security for traveling diplomats. The security fell to the marines and the civilian American security guards at the embassy.

I was to travel with American ambassador Donald Finn one fine summer day to the north of Afghanistan to meet with some of their most notorious, but cooperative, Northern Alliance warlords. Ambassador Finn planned to use me as one of his bargaining chips. He had certain diplomatic demands to make entailing cooperation between different Afghan factions, who historically fought each other. He hoped that by offering the prospect of humanitarian assistance for the Afghan families, he could sweeten the pot. My greatest concern was to get the Afghans' commitment and cooperation in providing security for humanitarian workers before funding programs that took aid workers to some of the most remote and wild places in the mountains of the region. These Afghan generals controlled much of the territory not under Taliban rule, so it was necessary to get their approval for any strangers to enter their regions. Ambassador Finn had a planned agenda with specific objectives to focus on. He was a skilled negotiator. My job was to sit quietly until he motioned to me, and then I would tell those we were meeting with about the humanitarian assistance available for the civilians. Of course we could not bring in assistance if the safety of the humanitarian workers was not guaranteed.

As the ambassador and I planned our meetings, it seemed as if they would come off rather like a novice vaudeville team: he'd speak and then—ta da—I'd come in with my punch line. We laughed about it as we discussed the setup, and he instructed me on what he needed.

I might have felt more intimidated, except that I knew from our time working together at the embassy in Kabul and seeing how he treated others that I could depend on receiving both encouragement and support from Ambassador Finn. He was a seasoned diplomat and a generous boss. He was serious and skillful when negotiating but full of fun when off duty. This made him delightful to work and travel with. Our trip promised to be very interesting.

Our day began with an early morning helicopter ride to the north, which meant getting up by four thirty to arrive at the helicopter location by a quarter to six for boarding. The security situation made this form of travel necessary. The roads were in such poor condition that the risk of an accident was very real, and the possibility of attack could not be ruled out. So we traveled in a US military helicopter.

It was a wonderful way to see the country. The day was clear and full of promise. The weather was nice, and the travel would be in the unpolluted mountain air that only a country unburdened with factories or industry can offer. Our group was made up of the ambassador, an American translator, a US Army Ranger colonel, and me, besides the helicopter crew. For those who have never flown in a helicopter, it is noisy, making conversation very difficult and usually reduced to hand gestures when shouting didn't work. The crew have speaker helmets, but these are very expensive and not necessary or provided for passengers. We flew low enough to make out many important landmarks. We all looked in wonder at the changing topography below us and motioned when there was something of interest for others to see. On the trip north, we flew over the beautiful Panjshir Valley, home of General Ahmad Massoud, the Lion of Panjshir and the most famous and beloved leader of the Northern Alliance in Afghanistan. We saw the remnants of the long Soviet war: destroyed buildings, burned-out orchards, and a countryside littered with rusted, bombed, and demolished tanks. On the way back, we flew further to the west over Bamiyan and saw its lush green fields and its strikingly beautiful cerulean blue lake. We also got to see the gaping holes in the mountains where the famous third- and fifth-century AD statues of Buddha were blown up by the Taliban in an attempt to cleanse Afghanistan of what the Taliban perceived to be religious heresy. The destruction of these ancient, historic statues was filmed and caused a worldwide outcry. At the time, the Taliban's foreign minister, Wakil Ahmed Muttawakil, was reported as saying, "We are not against culture, but we don't believe in these things. They are against Islam." This occurred just six months before the World Trade Center attacks. We all felt the tragic loss of so much, including these historic, treasured statutes. It was a stark reminder of why we were there. So while we were on an important mission, we still took advantage of the flight there and back to further experience the rich history of Afghanistan. I was both in my element negotiating humanitarian assistance and out of my element traveling with the ambassador and US military.

The helicopter's first touchdown was just outside the city of Kunduz, where we were to meet with General Mohammed Daud Daud. One of the local translators told me that General Daud was affectionately called "the baby general" because of his youth and round, babyish face. He had been trusted by General Massoud, who, before his death, put Daud in charge of protecting Kunduz. Massoud, trained as an architect but forced by circumstances to blow things up and spend the majority of his adult life fighting against the Soviet invasion, had been killed by a suicide bomber pretending to be a cameraman during a rare interview two days prior to 9/11. Now, just seven months after Massoud's murder, General Daud was following the orders of his fallen leader. He displayed the commitment and dogged faithfulness found in so many of the Afghan fighters. In November

2001, he had won a decisive battle, partnering with a small contingent of US Special Forces and CIA against thousands of Taliban. General Daud captured hundreds of prisoners, a rarity in most Afghan battles since fighters were either killed in the battle or escaped. These Taliban prisoners had been taken to Mazar-i-Sharif to a prison in the center of the city under the control of General Dostum, who was also on our meeting agenda for later that day.

But the first planned Afghan meeting was to be with the baby general, who had secured the city of Kunduz for the United Islamic Front for the Salvation of Afghanistan (Northern Alliance). He was the commander of the Kunduz Military Division and was considered a major leader with excellent battlefield skills, in spite of his youth. He was predicted to be a man with an important and powerful future. General Daud, like many young Afghan men, had only known war. At thirty-two years old, he had been fighting since his teen years in the 1980s. He was only a few years older than my second son—the son who had survived the World Trade Center attack. It made me see him in a different light. As so often happened, my personal situation came flashing back to me at surprising moments when I was in Afghanistan. Here was a connection that pierced my heart as I thought of General Daud and my son Jason being that close in age but with very different backgrounds. Here I was, meeting one because of what happened to the other.

I knew much of his personal history before being introduced to him and was eager to meet this Afghan man with deep roots in war and intrigue.

Our helicopter landed in a remote, dry, brown dirt field. The helicopter's whirling blades kicked up a thick cloud of dust that obstructed our view when exiting the craft. The rotors continued to whirl as we exited, and it was necessary for me to secure my hijab so it would not get caught up in the blades. Hunkered down, eyes and nose shielded, I hurried off the helicopter and rushed immediately to our waiting vehicles about a hundred feet from the aircraft. It was never good to be exposed in the open for long.

The first order of business was to make a stop at an American forward-operating base, known as an FOB, where US Marines would give us a classified briefing. The marines based in Kunduz knew the area and the players. They also knew the mood of the day regarding the locals and what we might expect or what might prove to be a risk to us. The locals would be surprised to see foreigners moving about in our large armored vehicles that had been forward positioned for our use.

The marines' base turned out to be a small, nondescript house located on a side street of the town with a two-foot-high mud-brick wall surrounding it. The front porch had mixed tiles for a floor, broken steps leading up to the front door, and a gray marble-like tile exterior. It looked like any other house on the town's street except for the sandbags stacked around the porch for protection. The marines told us that they had not yet had time to complete the sandbagging around the entire house. The inside rooms were sparsely furnished with olive green cots, a few locally purchased chairs, and lots of military equipment, including MRE brown boxes and duffle bags stacked against the walls. There was a central room for the group to gather in and three or four side rooms that served as bedrooms and additional storage space for supplies. We noted the curiosity of the local Afghans regarding everything that went on behind the short walls of this "American" house.

The marines briefed us about the situation in the region and about the politics of the local officials. Most of this had little to do with me beyond understanding what the stability of an area was and how it might affect our access to provide humanitarian assistance. I was not involved in any of the local political discussions or strategy for providing or improving military security.

I was the first American woman the marines had seen in weeks, maybe months. This turned out to be a real thrill for them. As an American woman, I represented a bit of home. I reminded them of wives, girlfriends, mothers, or sisters. They were surprised to see me there and wondered at my job. It was obvious by my dress that I was not in the military. I could hear the buzz of comments behind hands. "What is a woman like you doing here?" was a frequent question I was asked by both Americans and Afghans. Early in the war the US military personnel were still learning about the US civilian functions and services for the local noncombatants in war zones. But at this moment, it was fun for them to talk to an American woman who appeared in their little mud house in that remote location of Afghanistan. I was a novelty in their otherwise rather routine days.

The first official meeting was scheduled for thirty minutes after the briefing at the marines' safe house. Since we had that half hour, I asked one of the American translators if he would send someone to the market to buy a white burqa for me. I was surprised to see the women wearing white in this region since all I had seen up to that point were the pale blue burqas worn by the women in Kabul, which seemed to be the standard there. I had not seen the white before and wanted one to take back with me. It was to be my *first* new garment of the day. While it was important to stay on schedule, I was told that there was time for one of the Afghan men to run to the nearby market and buy this for me without creating any delay.

During my briefing for the day, I was told by the ambassador's security detail that they were there for *him*. I was not their responsibility. Jeff, a big, burly security guard, said, "Ma'am, if you want to be protected, it is your responsibility to get under the umbrella."

"What umbrella?" I asked. This was the first I had heard of any umbrella.

Jeff calmly explained, "This is what we call the circle of protection over and around the ambassador. It is how we surround him, shield him, and clear the way for him. You are outside of this."

So unlike the insurance commercials at home, apparently I was neither in good hands nor under a red umbrella of protection. Having been so informed, my protection was to be my quick wits and my ability to hover close by their mythical umbrella, or stay far away from whatever danger they might face. I wondered, if the ambassador was a potential target, was I safer under the umbrella next to him or was I safer keeping my distance from him? I generally opted for staying as close as possible with the hope that, like the missiles often shot at the embassy, the hostile action would miss him. At least if there was a threat and I was near the ambassador, his protection teams might knock me out of the way of danger as they protected the ambassador. This was all new for me.

I accepted the terms of travel for the day, and we were on our way. I needed to be quick on my feet to keep up with the tall, well-protected ambassador and his athletically fit protection detail. I had convinced myself that I would scurry all day to stay under that darn imaginary umbrella.

Every time the vehicle stopped, the security team got out, heads turning left, right, up, and down as they scanned the perimeter. They cleared the surrounding area, then opened the door for the ambassador and moved him forward quickly. Meanwhile, I was still trying to get out the other side of the car—the street side, I might add—attempting to maintain some semblance of dignity as well as my head covering while grabbing my notebook and my purse. Then I ran around the vehicle to catch up with that rapidly moving protection umbrella. I began to feel like the kid nobody wanted around. I knew it was not personal; I was just not that important. This was a hard reality to accept when traveling in diplomatic convoys—rank had privilege as well as responsibility. I had neither the rank nor the privilege but also much less responsibility for the day's outcome. My job was to stay alive and be ready to jump when the ambassador said to. My personal favorite goal was to stay alive for the day.

And so it went, all day long: me getting out the traffic side of the car, running around to the pedestrian side, and trying to catch up with the quickly moving phalanx of men heading into a building. My head cover kept slipping. My notebook and pen needed to be clasped firmly. My eyes were supposed to be cast downward at all times, and my clothes were sticking to me in the dust and heat. I wondered, what would my friends back home think of me now? How was it that I was meeting with ambassadors and warlords and ducking for cover whenever there was a loud noise? *Whose life was I living?*

At ten o'clock that morning, we arrived at General Daud's compound, a group of buildings nestled in a private area of Kunduz. Again, I was trying to keep up with the ambassador and his umbrella as we hurried to get inside. We entered a building on the left and walked down a long entry hall with dusty, scuffed wooden floors that echoed with each step. As we neared the end of the hall, we turned left and went into a meeting room, about fifteen feet wide by thirty feet long. The floor was covered with colorful, deep-red, patterned carpets that were traditional in Afghanistan. Tucked tightly against the walls were velvet, overstuffed sofas in a variety of colors and patterns. The light filtered in through dirty windows outlined by heavy red drapes. Standing at the far end of the room was General Daud, greeting each guest and speaking through a stiff and stilted translator. He shook hands with each man as he passed by him but was startled when I was presented to him. He did not reach out to shake my hand, as that would be a breach in etiquette. He would never reach for a woman's hand, even a Western woman's hand, unless she offered her hand to him first. I did not do so. I touched no one, and no one touched me.

General Daud took his official place in the back corner of the room next to a side table crowded with knickknacks, telephones, and some bowls of fruits and nuts. The ambassador sat on the other side of the corner table closest to the general. The five Afghan military staff in attendance positioned themselves along the wall to the right of the general, and the American translator and military personnel sat along the left side of the ambassador. Again, I was left to fend for myself. Where did I fit in? The obvious answer was nowhere. Seeing my moment of confusion, the polite US lieutenant colonel in our group invited me to come over and sit next to him. This put me almost directly across the room from General Daud, where I could look him squarely in the face. The ambassador's security detail stood both inside and outside the door to maintain control of the space and to make sure they were aware of anything happening outside.

Meeting General Daud was a bit of a shock. He had a larger-than-life reputation but was, in fact, a small man in stature. He was painfully thin, with baggy, olive green military trousers. He had a shock of beautiful, pure black hair surrounding his smoothly shaven round face. The lack of a beard was notable since most men in Kabul still wore beards—a requirement of the Taliban. Maybe General Daud's clean-shaven face was in direct defiance of that Taliban rule. He was soft-spoken, which wasn't unusual for the Afghan men I had met. It was obvious that he was a respected and effective leader of the hardened resistant freedom fighters. He was polite and serious, and he appeared shy to me. As an ethnic Tajik, his ancestry could be traced back to Tajikistan, a former Soviet republic on the northeastern border of Afghanistan. He was considered one of the most powerful and important opponents of the Taliban. General Daud inherited the command, on the death of Massoud, of the elite Afghan Northern Alliance regiment, the 303 Pamir Corps, which came out of the Panjshir Valley. It had been the main, elite fighting force of General Massoud. Now they were under the command of the baby general sitting before me.

I listened to the discussion, of which I was not a part until the ambassador turned to me and said, "Now, Mrs. McIntyre will share what she can do for you." This was my cue to jump in and talk about our humanitarian programs and the hope of helping those in need. But prior to being called on, I had occupied myself perusing the room. I watched these men who had known nothing but war from an early age. Two things struck me: one, how young the general was compared to the others in the room, and two, that he had a bank of three phones next to him, one of which was a 1950s-era pink princess phone. General Daud excused himself for just a moment during the discussions to pick up this phone—no dialing—and began speaking in rapid-fire Dari, the language of the north, to the person on the other end. He was terse. I got the impression that he was ordering something to be done and confirming that it was understood. He nodded, and said, "Da, da," a leftover from the Soviet occupation during his youth that means "yes, yes" in Russian. It was not unusual to hear a smattering of Russian words peppered in the middle of sentences with the Urdu, Dari, or Farsi that was spoken in the northern half of Afghanistan.

Shortly after the phone call, the meeting was adjourned. Apparently the pink phone was the watered-down version of the infamous red hotline on the US president's desk in Washington. The juxtaposition of testosterone-laden presences and the pink princess phone struck me as comical—this soft-spoken man, who made life-and-death decisions, used the phone of choice of every teenage girl in America in the 1950s.

I wanted a photo of this historic meeting as it was taking place. It would be impossible for me to take out my camera and snap photos, so I asked the good colonel sitting next to me if he would take a photo from his vantage point. Since there had been a few other photos snapped by the general's men to document the occasion, the colonel agreed. And so, captured for all posterity, was the pink princess phone at the ready next to the thin, baby-faced general of Kunduz.

117

As the general stood, he turned to shake hands and I saw him from behind. I noticed that his trousers were too big and that his belt had gathered the excess waistband into puckers at his back. It made him look vulnerable.

I studied the young general and wondered what he would have made of my thoughts, but they were mine to keep. I wished him well. In any other place, he would have been a polite, intelligent young man who would surprise people with his leadership skills and please young women with his dashing good looks. But on that day, in that place, he was a commander of troops and a military strategist with respect from both the local and international players in Afghanistan's newest war.

A decade later, on May 28, 2012, General Mohammed Daud Daud was assassinated in Kabul in retaliation for the Americans' killing of Osama bin Laden in Pakistan.

Chapter 16

The Black Fishnet Dress

It was customary for a host to present his guests with gifts in honor of their visit. And so as we rose to leave General Daud's meeting, he turned to his aides, who had come into the room with arms full of packages. He handed the packages, one at a time, to each of the men present at the meeting. Finally he had one package left, which he took and brought to me. It was not wrapped as the other gifts were. It had been handed to him by a man who had hurried into the room a few minutes before.

Now I thought I knew what the important call on the pink phone had been about during the meeting. I guessed that it was because he had gifts for all the men but nothing for the unexpected woman in the delegation. Something must have been found in the market quickly and brought back to him. I wondered at the buzz this request must have created in the outside room. I imagined the response: "Yes, General, I will get something immediately for you to present to the woman."

The unknown *mujahideen,* usually charged with capturing territory or killing someone, had to go shopping for a gift for a woman. I could imagine his chagrin as he turned to his compatriots, saying, "What do I get an American woman?" I imagined a couple of them rushing to the market to see what it had to offer. They would surely look for something special, something unique. As they hunted, something caught their eyes. It was just the gift for me—that unique something that was perfect for the baby general's guest, the American woman.

"How kind of you," I said. "Should I open it now?" I was unsure of the protocol but saw that the men had ripped into their gifts, so I did the same.

I opened the brown paper covering tied with string from the local market. Inside, I found a shiny black garment. As I removed it, it caught the attention of those around the room. The seasoned fighters' eyes lit up as they saw my gift. I had just gotten my *second* garment of the day.

It was a black fishnet dress. There could be found in local markets these rather provocative women's clothing that husbands would appreciate at home or that women might wear with other women. These clothes were usually out of view and had to be asked for by the men shopping. Apparently one of the militia-shoppers was savvy enough to know this and had asked, and found, this unique garment, not for his wife, but for the American woman.

It was shiny and black, with slits up each side seam to mid-thigh level.

I remembered Jamal's stories of the vivid imaginations of the Afghan men, denied even a fleeting glance at any woman who was not related to them, and now I was standing in a room full of strangers holding aloft nothing short of the most provocative garment I had ever seen in Afghanistan. Even by my more relaxed standards, it was risqué.

The Americans kept a straight face with some effort. I turned to General Daud. "Thank you for this amazing gift," I said. It was the truth when I said, "I have nothing like it and will treasure it. How very thoughtful of you to include me with this souvenir."

He smiled. His aides smiled. Apparently the gift was considered a success.

Once I was in the car with the ambassador, he turned to me and asked to see the dress again. I gave it to him. He inspected it closely. With a grin, he said, "I officially estimate this dress's value at less than thirty-five dollars. And so, you can keep it."

The occupants of the car broke into raucous laughter. I knew exactly what the ambassador had just done. By valuing the dress at less than thirty-five dollars, he had complied with the US government's ethical guidelines for accepting gifts while on assignment. Had the gift been worth more, I would have had to turn it over to the embassy as an official gift and not been allowed to keep it. My dress had just been cleared for me to keep forever. Lucky me!

"What makes the men there think I would wear such a dress?" I asked. "What about me screams, 'This is the perfect gift'—a slinky, black, fishnet dress with slit sides?" In fact, I had been working hard to be demure and submissive and present as a modest Muslim woman would throughout the trip in this very restrictive society. It appeared it had all been for naught if a black fishnet dress jumped out as the perfect gift for me.

Incidentally, the gifts for the men were small, beautifully made area carpets. Now *that* was a gift to get excited about!

There continued to be much speculation about the black dress as we went on with our busy day. We had places to go and people to meet, but under it all was good natured bantering about which event I should wear the black fishnet dress to at the embassy. I heard a lot of ribbing that I must, simply *must*, wear it to boost morale for the marines. It was a perfect foil for teasing as the day went forward.

Chapter 17

More Meetings

The day was only half over. We still had meetings with more generals: an ethnic Tajik, General Ustad Atta Mohammed Noor; and an ethnic Uzbek, General Abdul Rashid Dostum. It was, and is, important to know the ethnicity of various persons in Afghanistan. This is their primary source of identity. I was always surprised by this. Historical ethnicity seemed to mean so much to Afghans and had a rather strong influence on social strata and power. Rather than seeing each other as Afghans, they saw everyone according to ethnic background. I came to believe that this focus on ethnicity caused many of the problems between tribes. There seemed to be a genetically derived hatred of "the other" passed on from generation to generation. Everything seemed to be measured as a zero-sum game. If one group was honored, the other was not honored. I found it amazing that the Afghans seemed to rank the status of each individual according to ethnicity and would not recognize that all people, or tribes, could be good and all heritages could be rich. Instead, it was a matter of who was better than the other. Because of these sensitivities, we had to schedule separate meetings, hoping to bring the generals together later in the afternoon. There was an uneasy peace between the men borne of having a common enemy in the Taliban. Both of them were rather famous, or infamous, depending on one's view, for their bravery and viciousness in battle and their unwavering, dictatorial command over their troops and families during both the Soviet war and the subsequent civil war. They also had an unparalleled hatred for each other. The city of Mazar-i-Sharif had been split for decades between these men with a constant tug of war between the neighborhoods and streets.

I was frequently perplexed that Afghans could express such love and loyalty to their own specific tribes while espousing a rampant hatred of another. This same dynamic was often applied to the various Islamic religious sects. For those of us unconnected to such strong feelings, we need only to look back in our Western history to see the violent days of the Protestant Reformation period during the sixteenth century when the church encouraged the killing of people who were labeled heretics. This challenge to the authority in Catholic Europe is no different than what Islam is experiencing today as it struggles with lines of authority within its faith. The Reformation suffered through the Thirty Years' War with decades of unrest to follow. Is this a sign of what we can expect between Sunni and Shite sects within the Islamic faith of today? Does it foretell how long America should plan to be in Afghanistan? We would never have guessed so in the early days of 2002.

In order to get to the first of the two separate meetings, the first with General Atta Mohammed and the second with General Dostum, we had to fly. We headed to our waiting helicopter for a short, half-hour flight to Mazar-i-Sharif from our location in Kunduz. Once we arrived, armored cars again met us and drove us between the two compounds of the warring generals. At the meeting with General Atta Mohammed, I was quiet. General Atta Mohammed was a serious man, tall and lanky and dressed in military garb. He seemed uneasy with me there, unused to having a woman present during any important discussions on sensitive matters. The most important work of the day was the diplomatic dialogue geared toward engendering further cooperation between the two local leaders. The ambassador was masterful in his discussions and got the agreement from General Atta Mohammed that he would meet with General Dostum if Dostum agreed. This was quite a breakthrough and a great success for the ambassador.

As we left, General Atta Mohammed did a head count of our group and sent out an equal number of small carpets to be given to us as we drove away, so it looked like I was in for a carpet after all. These were given with little ceremony and with little graciousness. By the end of the day, I had decided that General Atta Mohammed, always referred to with the formal double name, was the coldest of the men I had met.

Next, we headed over to General Dostum's compound across town to move the negotiations further along. His compound was quite luxurious compared to anything else we had seen that day. He housed many of his troops around him, and it served, I was told, as a place of rest and relaxation for his troops fighting on the front, who rotated in on a schedule, and as a place to bring their families together. The grounds were well groomed with grass and flowers in abundance. There were many small, simple houses around a larger central building, which I learned belonged to General Dostum. His men served as compound guards while on R & R in this location.

We arrived in a convoy of black armored cars and were met by a brawny man in fatigues. He was short and stocky, which I noticed was a common physique among the Uzbeks. He led us to the general's quarters. After we were escorted to the meeting room and seated around the room, General Dostum entered the room surrounded by his officers. I was beginning to appreciate the difference in posturing and hosting styles of the two generals. General Dostum played the home-court advantage to the hilt. It was no accident that we were brought in through the front gate, past the well-groomed grounds and numerous troops in full view. His grand entrance surrounded by his officers, after we were seated and therefore forcing us to stand as he entered, was also well staged. He was short and stocky like many of the soldiers I had seen outside. I found him to be quite intimidating with his head of thick, wiry, gray hair; large black mustache; and heavy black brows. He was in civilian clothes, which surprised me. Still, he had a menacing, threatening look about him. I am not sure if I was becoming fanciful as the day wore on, but he was nicknamed "the butcher of the North" for a reason, and I believed it fit him well. He both frightened me and awed me. He probably would have been pleased to know that. Stories abounded about the vicious manner in which he would kill his enemies and prisoners. I was secretly glad that I did not need to shake hands with this man who had so much blood on them.

Ambassador Finn again handled the meeting with finesse and skill. He was able to finalize negotiations for the agenda points that we needed from General Dostum in his compound and his area of control within the city and also to gain agreement from Dostum that he would meet with his rival, General Atta Mohammed. Our interpreter called on behalf of Ambassador Finn, rather than General Dostum, to invite General Atta Mohammed to come over for the meeting. Since they were only a few miles apart and General Atta Mohammed had been waiting for our call, the meeting was arranged for that very afternoon. What a success today would be for the ambassador!

I felt sure that General Dostum would use the occasion to intimidate his rival and to showcase his wealth and power. He did not disappoint.

The ambassador was a master of diplomatic poise as he maneuvered the two obstinate, powerful men to his position. It was a joy to watch him as he negotiated with both generals, making clear what America's position was and conveying our plans and hopes for Mazar-i-Sharif.

When the ambassador was ready for me to enter the conversation, he again indicated that I had something to offer the generals for getting along and safeguarding the humanitarian workers. I discussed the funding America was making available and how it could be used for the civilians in Mazar-i-Sharif. Again, I stressed the need for security and safety of the humanitarian workers. In order for this to happen, both generals had to assure me, and the ambassador, that there would be no threat on the humanitarian staff from either of the two militia groups and that the generals would confirm control of their troops. They did this, and I told them I would begin to work with partners in Kabul to set up programs in Mazar-i-Sharif. They were pleased.

Throughout the meetings, the two Afghan generals looked at me with some disdain, but they listened as I spoke. I am quite sure that they were surprised to find that I was a contributing member of the delegation.

The ambassador listened attentively and respectfully to my comments. I appreciated his modeling respect for me and for my contribution to the meeting. I was pleased also that I had prepared well for the meeting and spoken clearly and with authority about the humanitarian situation in Mazar-i-Sharif.

I addressed the generals directly, saying, "I know there are more than six thousand families in dire need here. The poverty is on both sides of the city. I have heard that there is widespread hunger among civilians. Please let me be clear: I can bring in some food, but more importantly, I want to bring in some programs to put people back to work. I am hoping that this can include women in the work program so that they may earn money also. I am especially concerned about the widows who have no man to support them." At this point, the generals nodded to the ambassador. It was noteworthy that they did not nod to me.

I continued, "In order to bring any programming to the city, I need to be assured that each of you will inform your troops of humanitarian workers in the area and safeguard them."

As I presented my program, I saw a change in both General Atta Mohammed and General Dostum. They leaned forward and appeared to show respect for my situational knowledge and for the potential amount of funding that could come to their city. Both generals knew that an unhappy public was a weak platform for their winning further approval and maintaining control. I was not taking sides, only presenting what was possible within the city at large.

They both assured the delegation and me that security would not be a problem for the humanitarian workers. It would be safe for them to come north. I was thrilled by this commitment. And I must say, I basked just a little in the admiration of the ambassador and military escorts who were present. I think I did myself proud that day.

General Atta Mohammed hurried out at the end of the meeting. He and his small contingent of men were not keen on dallying in an enemy's camp. General Dostum suddenly became the all-gracious host and escorted us out. He even agreed to have his photo taken with the ambassador and with me. He was full of bravado and confidence, having hosted such a momentous meeting. The photo op was conveyed as a bit of an honor for me. I think I might have made a small dent in his impression of American women and the power that we can have.

As we were leaving, I commented on how I was feeling, and the US lieutenant colonel with us told me a story. In November 2001, prisoners in the nineteenth-century prison fortress, Qala-i-Jangi, located in the center of Mazar-i-Sharif, rioted. Many hardened, Taliban fighters had been transferred to this prison from the battle at Kunduz, where they had been captured. In the chaotic process, prisoners had smuggled weapons into the prison, which they later turned on the guards once inside. The riot quickly got out of control, so the lieutenant colonel told General Dostum that he could have a US military jet fly overhead and bomb the prison in a way that would allow for external access. Dostum asked if it was possible for the pilot to be so accurate, showing some surprising concern for the civilian population around the prison and also for his troops nearby. The lieutenant colonel took great pleasure in telling him that not only could the pilot be so accurate, but the pilot was also a woman.

Dostum could not believe his ears. Surely the US government wouldn't entrust such an expensive and sophisticated weapon to the hands of a woman. And surely no woman could learn how to fly such a plane. So the lieutenant colonel radioed up and let Dostum speak to the pilot. Sure enough, it was a woman. He was amazed. The shock on his face was a Kodak moment missed. But this turned out to be a very sad day. It was the day of the first deaths of Americans on Afghan soil. These were the brave CIA agents who entered the prison to negotiate with the prisoners and never came out alive. They were killed, it is believed, by the prisoners prior to the bombing.

Dostum got on his radio and called into the prison. He told the Taliban that if they did not give up, he would have the prison bombed from above and they would all come to an ignoble end from being bombed by a female pilot. It was the ultimate insult—death at the hands of a woman. Dostum nicknamed her the Angel of Death. It was so in character with Dostum. He liked to inflict as much suffering as possible on his enemy, even psychological, while performing his job. It gave him extra pleasure that the Taliban would be horrified at a death in battle at the hands of a woman.

It is unclear whether the Taliban believed him or not, but they did not surrender. The bombing was ordered, and the prison was hit. Dostum's troops and the American soldiers were able to enter the prison and regain control, all thanks to a woman. How the lieutenant colonel liked to tell that story. I could not know the pilot's name, but she was famous among the Dostum troops and continued to be referred to only as the Angel of Death.

And so I had just gained the attention of General Abdul Rashid Dostum, a terrifying soldier, the "butcher of the north," in a much more modest manner than the brave female pilot. But for me, of course, it was in a civilized meeting in the midst of an unholy alliance.

Six weeks after starting humanitarian programming in the north, one of the foreign aid workers was attacked and raped by a small militia group. All programming stopped.

Chapter 18

The Blue Mosque

As we wound down a day of intense and successful meetings, we began our drive out of Mazar-i-Sharif. We caravanned slowly through the old streets of the city, which gave the impression of a historic caravan route with so many people on foot leading animals loaded with goods. We generally felt quite satisfied with our work for the day. There was a lot of talk about getting back to the embassy in Kabul, writing up reports, and acting on the information gathered and promises made.

As we were driving, still in the center of the city, the ambassador suddenly shouted, "Stop here!" He was twisting in his seat, looking backward at the mosque we had just passed. With awe in his eyes and a sense of some private revelation, he said, almost to himself, "I've read so much about the Blue Mosque, and there it is. I have to stop. I just have to. We cannot drive past without going in to see this national historic treasure."

And so the car stopped on the side of the road, which was a real security risk. Most driving was done at breakneck speed, if possible, to move through any potential danger as quickly as possible. And now here we were, stopped on a paved street that posed a myriad of threats. The area was lined with trees, and sitting about fifty yards back from the road was this magnificent mosque. In spite of its size, it would have been missed as we sped by had it not been for the ambassador's knowledge of its presence in the city. Thanks to the ambassador's quick recognition, we were now parked in front of one of the most holy sites for Muslims in Afghanistan.

A little bit of history: the mosque was completed in 1481, before Columbus sailed for America. And yet, in this remote place in the East, often thought of as backwards and associated with tragedy, stands this glorious shrine to honor Ali ibn Abi Talib (Hazrat Ali), a cousin and son-in-law of the Prophet Muhammad (PBUH). (Note: Writing the name of the Prophet Muhammad requires the honorific "Peace Be Upon Him" (PBUH) in respect for the Islamic faith.) The Shi'a Muslims believe that Iman Ali's remains were in Najaf, Iraq, but the Sunnis believe that his remains were transferred to the Blue Mosque to prevent them from being desecrated by enemies. According to local folklore, Ali's remains were brought here on a white camel. It is an important site honored by millions of Muslims around the Islamic world.

The compound is made up of many buildings. Side galleries offer places for private worship or honoring other, lesser figures in Islam and local political or military heroes. The entire inner courtyard is paved with white marble tiles that reflect the day's sunlight and the evening's lamplight. Centered in this acre of white marble is the beautiful main building of sea blue, turquoise, yellow, and white ornate tiles, creating archways all around. It looks like many of the tiles have flowers painted on them, but on closer inspection, we saw that they were made up of multiple smaller tiles creating a flowered pattern. The many domes are of a stunning bright blue. To the left and right in the courtyard are absolution stations—one for men and one for women—where the faithful wash their feet, hands, and faces as instructed in the Quran prior to entering to pray before Allah.

Once we paused to really look at this shrine, we could easily see that it dominated the skyline of Mazar-i-Sharif. That day, and for centuries before, it was the most important landmark in the city. There was no convincing the ambassador that he could not get a closer look.

The security detail was apoplectic at the notion of this unscheduled stop. They looked at the ambassador like he was crazy. I sat quietly in the mix of the heated discussion about the merits versus the risks of stopping here.

"This is not on our agenda, sir, and we haven't cleared this site for a stop," Malcolm said. A muscled thirty-something African American with years of experience, Malcolm was head of the ambassador's security team.

"It's not possible to deviate from our plan. This is a highly sensitive site that is unprotected. I just cannot approve this stop. What is so important about this place?"

The ambassador, an Eastern scholar, was ready to answer that question, but rather than dwelling on the historic merits of the site, he addressed the primary concern of the security team. "No one is waiting here to hurt me. It is safe exactly because it is an unplanned stop." The ambassador turned to the driver. "Park right here in front." The poor driver, one of the security team, was caught in the middle. Should he listen to Malcolm, his direct supervisor, or to the ambassador, the ultimate boss? The car pulled over further and parked by the curb. The entire entourage followed suit. Out jumped the ambassador from our car, quickly followed by his security team. They immediately formed a circle around him, and the umbrella moved forward. I was not going to be left behind. I jumped out of my side and ran around to catch up with the men charging forward.

The vehicles in our convoy behind began to empty of their occupants as the rest of the security team fanned out. No one was happy about this stop except the ambassador, who was excited about seeing this historic site. *Mazar-i-Sharif* means "noble shrine," and here it was sitting right in front of us, a treasure too good to pass up.

I heard the ambassador say, "We have to go inside." The security detail acquiesced after some audible groans. They did establish one concession, or so they thought: that going inside depended on whether they saw anything suspicious. If so, we would immediately turn back to the car. Everyone—and by *everyone*, I mean the ambassador—agreed.

The heavily armed guards did a cursory review of the outside of the site and then continued to whisk the ambassador toward the entrance to the shrine. Again, I was left behind. With some difficulty, I caught up to them just before reaching that entrance.

The usual holy men and guards were working in front of the shrine and stopped our little delegation. The ambassador's eyes were full of expectation, while the security team's eyes were full of dread. Two things immediately became clear—first, we had to remove our shoes, a common practice prior to entering any mosque, and second, the protection team could not enter with their weapons. They were told by the local men positioned at the doorway to hand over the weapons. Each of the ambassador's security team must have had three or four weapons on his body—the muscle under the umbrella. We were at somewhat of an impasse. This demand presented a major problem to security, as they *never* relinquish their weapons.

But the ambassador had not come this close to give up. He insisted that it would be okay to go in. The mosque guards looked very concerned. The protection detail had to deal with a determined ambassador yet could not cause a scandal by disrespecting Islamic protocol. In the end, they turned to me. Yes, to me—the red-headed stepchild no one needed to protect.

"Sue, you go in and stay next to the ambassador," growled Malcolm. "If anything looks amiss, immediately call out to us and we *will* come in to get him." I noted that even under this new arrangement, I was not the one they would come to rescue.

Aha, so now, the persona non grata of under-the-umbrella protection was asked to go in and *protect* the ambassador. It was a point not missed by any of us.

The ambassador looked expectantly at me. I agreed.

"And if anything looks suspicious, what am I to do?" I asked.

"Just run out and get us," responded one of the team.

"Okay, I'll do what I can," I said. But I could not resist adding, "But remember, I am not armed, I have no training, and I am, after all, just a woman." I felt it was necessary to make these points clear now that I was to be responsible for this lovely man, our ambassador. He just smiled. I am sure that the Afghan guards at the door of the shrine wondered what all this talk was about.

Everyone agreed to the plan, and off came our shoes. As we entered the mosque, I looked back to see the very nervous security team shifting their weight in anticipation of any danger. I felt sure that no one was going to be allowed to enter the mosque while we were inside and that those already inside would pose our only threat—and they didn't know we were coming.

It was an amazing opportunity to enter this very holy shrine of the Afghans. The ambassador gave me a brief history lesson as we walked around. He was good about staying right with me or letting me stay right beside him. I looked left and right vigilantly, praying for no disturbances. Actually, I tried to remember that no one knew who we were or why we were there. He was just a tall white foreigner with a nervous woman walking around behind him, and I was properly covered.

We paused in front of the tomb in the center of the chamber. It hit me: this was the tomb of the cousin and son-in-law of the Prophet Muhammad.

My busy thoughts settled on what an amazing day I was having. I had met with three of the most dominant warlords of Afghanistan, sat through delicate negotiations, and witnessed two hostile and powerful warlords come together and discuss how to rule their city. Now I was protecting the ambassador inside of a holy mosque. There would be moments throughout my assignment in Afghanistan when I would have moments like this, which seemed to feel more like adventure touring rather than working on life-and-death issues. I guessed that there would be few dull days.

As we circled around the tomb and headed back toward the exit, the ambassador got a twinkle in his eye. "Sue, you go out just before me," he said. "I'll lag behind just a few seconds. Let's see what the protection team does."

My first thought was, *Holy shit, he cannot mean this.* I was horrified.

"You have to be kidding me," I said, aghast. "They will shoot me first and then come charging in to find you. Don't ask me to do this. I beg you."

With a small smile, the ambassador assured me he would be immediately behind me. How could anyone refuse this man?

So, out I went. As expected, within a nanosecond the protection team was all over me. "Where's the ambassador?"

I looked momentarily stunned and said, "Isn't he behind me?" It's hard to describe how many emotions can run over a face in a split second. Horror, fear, and anger were among the first that I saw on the faces of the security team. It was a moment of sheer agony for them before the ambassador strolled out, in all innocence, with a big smile on his face. Such a prankster! I was just glad to still be standing and unhurt. The team immediately surrounded the ambassador, forgot about me in their high adrenaline state, and practically pushed the ambassador toward the waiting car. I trailed behind, wondering about the tongue-lashing I would get when back in the safety of the car. There is little humor with protection teams when the person being protected disappears.

When we were back in the car, the ambassador stood up for me and owned that it was his prank. What the heck, the ambassador had his little bit of fun after a day of hard work.

We ended our stay in the ancient city on this note of unexpected sightseeing. But for me, the day was more than this last-minute adventure. I had sat with and talked with two of the most powerful and feared men in Afghanistan. They would forever have a place in Afghanistan history and lore. I had introduced them, maybe for the first time, to a woman of position and influence—and a woman with the power of the purse strings, at least so far as the humanitarian response went.

I carried home my black fishnet dress and carpets as physical reminders of the day but doubted I would ever forget the time I touched history.

Chapter 19

The Women and Children of Kabul

A lot of my work involved monitoring programs after the initial assessments were funded and completed. One of the critical programs in Kabul focused on support for women, especially the widows. Without a doubt, these women were among the neediest in Afghanistan. The Taliban, with its conservative and ultra-restrictive rules concerning women, forbade a woman to enter the streets without a man. This was like a death sentence for widows without sons, brothers, or fathers. How were they to shop? What about working to earn money? Medical care? All of these were out of reach for widows, especially those with small children. In accordance with Afghan tradition, once married, a woman belonged to her husband and, in the event of his death, to his family. Her family would rarely step in to assist her. If her husband's family was not particularly fond of her, she was left on her own after his death and his property went to his family. If she was lucky, his family would allow her to continue living in her own home; if not, she would be put out on the street. Her children might be taken away if her husband's family wanted them. Often the girls were not considered to have any value, so only the boys would be taken.

Much of a widow's life was a battle to stay alive, for both herself and whatever children she had left. The deceased husband's family had all the power.

After the US and Northern Alliance defeat of the Taliban, we found many widows suffering in deplorable condition. It was not unusual to enter a poor apartment or shelter and find a woman who had not left her home for months, maybe years. She could be living in complete and abject poverty, dependent on the kindness of neighbors and strangers. The living arrangements most often consisted of one room, no plumbing, and only an earthen fire pit for cooking. The sight never failed to move me. The women and children were inevitably in rags, very dirty, skinny, and sick. I could not imagine why a society would do this to so many of its people. Young children, whether boys or girls, could go out, so from a very early age they were taught to forage for food. If there was a young boy, even as young as six or seven, he could accompany his mother out and be her protection if they came across the Taliban patrolling the streets. It never made sense to me, but the young son could escort her out as the ranking male of the household.

Early assistance usually consisted of feeding them, getting health care as needed, and beginning some social services for the families. But continual charity was not practical and so was not a long-term solution. The women, many of whom were very young mothers whose husbands had been fighters, had no education. The older women often had an education from the former Soviet days in Kabul when women had attended universities. But for the young mothers this was not the case. With two, three, or more babies, these women were lost, frightened, illiterate, and without rights.

We started funding programs with the UN World Food Program (WFP) to use the existing skills of the women. We started what became known as the widows' bakeries. We provided flour, salt, and other ingredients so they could make the simple bread of the Afghans. The hope was that they would not only have bread for themselves but also be able to sell extra loaves at market so that they could buy other much-needed supplies. Since our program provided money to buy the stoves and rent space for cooking, there was no overhead cost, allowing for as much profit as possible for these desperate women.

On one of my morning trips into Kabul, I went to review some of the bakery programs and planned to talk with the women. I left the embassy with my driver and some of the other team members around eight in the morning. The roads were already a tangled mess of cars, trucks, animals and people, and the heat was rising, along with the dust kicked up by the presence of all the activity. We picked our way through the twisted, broken streets, most of which were unpaved. It was going to be another dirty, dusty day.

The bakeries were placed in out-of-the-way locations on corners of back streets in order to provide the women with as much privacy and protection as possible. They were reluctant to be out and seen working in any of the main shopping areas. As we drove to the various bakeries, we often had to negotiate our vehicles over piles of sand and dirt, presumably to be used someday for paving the roads. Much of these haphazard construction sites were the remnants of previous Kabul city or neighborhood plans to improve the streets. Now they were just more debris to negotiate. That "someday" was often decades or more away, but the piles stood in tribute to the hope of a better future.

Approaching the work sites was a tactical feat, involving maneuvering the vehicles around neighborhoods full of activity. It was not unusual for WFP to collaborate with the neighborhood residents to bring extra income to them, as well as the widows, by incorporating water and drainage repair and roadwork projects to the bakeries. This co-programming strategy often enhanced the acceptance of and support for one program, in this case widows' bakeries, by developing another one linked to the first. This particular road was about ten feet wide at most. As usual, all was chaotic with kids running around and dogs jumping and barking at vehicles. Broken-down cars were rusting on the sides of the road. Bicycles were circling by. Wheelbarrows half-filled from the previous day's work lined the sides of the narrow road, and men were clustered in groups or walked along the sides.

"The bakery is so far off the main shopping street. How do they get their business?" I asked one of the UNWFP workers.

"Most of the women take a number of loaves home and sell them in their neighborhoods. This helps the women who cannot leave their homes as the bread comes to them," she replied. "Even without that, they are all too shy to be on a main street and are afraid of being seen coming to work. The fear of retaliation is still strong, and they don't trust that the US and international community will be here forever to protect them. It is also why they still all wear the full-cover burqa. A face seen uncovered on the streets today will be recorded and remembered for a long time."

I nodded. "The women are so brave to come out at all, given their past experiences with the Taliban. It must all be so threatening for them."

"Many of the women are quite young and have only lived under the strict rules of the Taliban. Their young brothers are often the most domineering, now that their husbands have been killed in the war. It would not do for them to bring dishonor on their families by working without male permission or being seen on the streets alone. Yes, it is still very frightening for them to work, but the alternative is to die of hunger at home," my translator said.

"Let's go inside to talk to some of them," I suggested. I was eager to meet some of these brave young widows. I also wanted to complete my city work and get back to the embassy, where there was green grass and some shade even if there was no air conditioning. The day promised to be scorching.

We entered the small, primitive bakery. It had a dirt floor and gray unpainted walls of wood and cement. The room was about ten by twelve feet, a small space. There was no ventilation, no fans, no windows, and certainly no air conditioning in the stone and mud hut. Four women were pounding dough, rolling it, and tossing it on the sides of a primitive, cavernous metal oven. The heat generated by the coals glowing in the pit of the oven made for a sauna-like atmosphere. The women looked like ghosts, fragile and sprinkled with flour. The ceilings were low, and the heat was already overwhelming, even though it was early in the day.

"How can the women stand it for hours as they bake?" I asked.

"It's why they start at the dawn to work and finish by ten or eleven," the local worker explained. "Besides, the great opportunity to earn their own money and provide food for their children is well worth the discomfort to each of these women. You may ask them yourself how they feel about working."

I quickly took him up on this suggestion. Although very shy, one woman explained through the translator, "This is my lifeline. This feeds my children and gives me a few Afghanis (money) to buy essential things for my family. Thank you so much for helping us with this work."

I told her what I always said when people thanked me personally: "This money comes from the people of the United States, and you are very welcome to it. It is truly my joy to be able to bring this program to you with our UN partners." It was one of the greatest parts of my job to say that.

I was humbled by the women's gratitude toward us for giving them the most basic of help. In that miserable, hot, crowded, dusty bakery, they expressed appreciation and amazement that people far away, who did not know them, had given them money to live. These women did not know about 9/11, but they did know what it was to be abandoned, mistreated, and desperate.

I was the face of America for them. At that moment and in that bakery, they felt only gratitude and affection for me.

As I left the work site, the women were full of shy smiles. They usually covered their mouths when smiling so as not to look too forward but also because many were missing teeth, decayed from poor nutrition or knocked out from a beating by a male relative. My heart always broke a little each time I saw a damaged face. I offered the women warm hugs, something sorely lacking in their lives. For these Afghan women, I could see that a hug was an amazing thing. Hugging was frivolous in the everyday struggle to survive and certainly not to be found in most homes. Even when husbands were present, I was told, interactions between husbands and wives were few and kept to the essential.

But I thought hugs were essential. I gave them often to the women and children I encountered.

On another day, my trip into Kabul included hosting a congressional delegation, better known among diplomats as a codel. I was to meet the team at a hospital where we were funding a feeding program for malnourished children. In order to qualify for entry to the hospital program, the children were rather far along in the starvation process and near death. The most heart-wrenching of them had the big-eyed, skeletal look most Westerners have seen on TV. It upset me so much to see these children in such bad condition, but I thought that visiting this hospital program was important for understanding the dire conditions of civilians in Afghanistan. This codel from Washington was in Kabul for only one day due to the high security risks. Included in the group was my friend and congressman, Robin Hayes, from North Carolina. He and his team were to meet me at the hospital, where I was scheduled to take them through the newly opened emergency-feeding ward and introduce them to the Afghan doctors and nurses. This was a really important day for me, as it was the first time someone I knew from home would see my work in Afghanistan or, for that matter, any foreign country where I have worked.

As usual, the schedule was tight. Codels, like ambassadorial trips, were timed to the minute. I was to be on the hospital steps by exactly 1:15 p.m. The delegation had exactly forty minutes at the hospital to greet the hospital director, meet staff, and go to the feeding ward to see some of the children.

"Good afternoon," I greeted the group as they arrived. To my friend Robin I said, "Welcome to my world. It is amazing to me that you are here to see what I do and how I work when away from home. I hope this will bring into focus my job and help you to share this work back home in North Carolina, as well as in Washington."

"Sue, it is so good to see you here. And look at you, all covered up and submissive," he joked. I was in one of my Afghan shalwar kameez outfits with a hijab circled around my head and over my shoulders. By then I was so used to wearing them that I hadn't thought about it being a novelty to Robin to see me this way.

Robin had celebrated Christmas with my family and met my children. I was definitely being seen in a new light today. "Yes, I'm behaving here, but I'm still myself underneath, so don't expect any changes back home when I next see you." He knew that *submissive* was not a term that generally applied to me.

The hospital tour began. It was always a bit of a shock to see the stripped-down halls of health-care facilities in developing countries. This was no different, except that the area was dingier and darker than usual. People needing care sat on the floor in the halls patiently awaiting their turn. There were no waiting rooms and certainly no coffee shops or receptionists to offer a cold drink of water. It was hot and, as always, dusty, both in and out of the building. The elevators didn't work, so we climbed three flights of stairs to get to the children's ward. There was no smell of the astringent that Westerners associate with hospitals, which means a lack of sanitation. There was no running water, no running toilets, and certainly no disinfectant used in the course of the day. We bypassed the adults' wards, given our constraints on time, and headed straight to the children's ward.

About twenty children were lying lethargically in broken, rusty metal cribs. They ranged in age from three to four months old to maybe six or seven years old. It was hard to tell their ages, especially with the older children, who were so small from malnourishment that their growth was stunted. This would not change even with better nutrition since some developmental needs cannot be made up for later. The sad state of these children made me feel uncomfortable in my and our group's robust health. I was embarrassed by the extra flesh on my bones. The children had the haunted look seen in those who are starving and no longer have enough energy left to cry or care. Their skin was parchment thin and so very dry, with a tinge of blue. It lay over their tiny, birdlike, bony contours in a pathetic, real-life caricature of skeleton drawings found in anatomy texts. I could only think how life had failed these little ones who were doomed from the moment of conception to eke out survival from whatever scraps life had left over for them. A despondent, slow withering of the spark of life was in their eyes. Guilt always weighed heavily on my soul when I looked into the lost gaze of these children's eyes.

I could hear the muffled, horrified voices of the delegates as we walked deeper into the ward:

"There are so many children here."

"The ward is so dark and dismal."

"Many of these beds are broken."

"Many of the beds don't have sheets on them."

"Oh, my God, how thin they are!"

In truth, it was a miserable place. It was not a place for a sweet baby or curious toddler. But then, these children were barely alive and were not looking around. They had never seen a brightly colored mobile hanging over their cribs or a cheery painting on the wall. I feared that this gloomy ward was probably much like home—maybe even better.

"How tiny they are. They have such thin hair, and not one has a smile," Robin commented.

"They don't have the strength to waste on a smile. They're so malnourished that breathing and surviving are the most they can do right now," I said.

"I know. But it's heartbreaking to see the children this way."

"That's true. And these are the lucky ones," I said. "We found them and got them here for treatment and for food. So many children in the villages or hidden in tumbled-down buildings in Kabul will never be found. They will die." It was a depressing fact.

I saw pain on this good man's face, my friend from home. I felt tears in my eyes as I was again faced with my limitations. Suffering in such little ones was beyond my understanding. I was incensed. I was sad. I was frustrated.

I was eternally grateful for my life in America, where my children and grandchildren were safe and had nourishment, unlike these little ones.

I returned to the embassy feeling drained. As always, I was greeted by my friendly marines, who asked, "What's it like out there?"

How could I tell them? I did not want to explain Kabul to them that day.

Chapter 20

Alone

I had some bad days as I worked in Afghanistan. While I enjoyed my work and was fascinated by the country and its people, I had been away from my family since January 2002, almost five months now. I was lonely and tired. I wanted to be with people I loved and among things I knew.

Living in a high-stress situation began to change the focus of my life. This shifting was happening outside my conscious awareness. I was forgetting who I was. I was caught up in the daily tension of being in a war zone. It was easy to forget that the people I loved at home were still there for me. I felt alone. I felt sure that no one would understand what I was going through. All of this led to a distortion in what was real and what was not. Home was a lost dream.

As I observed others cope, I saw some of the same reactions I was having. It was impossible to work, live, and sleep with the same people day in and day out without developing close bonds. We hid from bombs together. We laughed in bathroom lines together. We grappled with the serious problems that we faced each day. And as the bonds grew, the threads of connections back home broke. Surely no one would understand or know me when I went home. Often I found myself asking where home was, with no answer. Where did I belong? I knew this was a common question among my colleagues. We were all human, and the need for shared experiences with loved ones was part of the glue that holds relationships together.

I watched as marriages were strained—some beyond repair. These were good people, but some had lost their way in foreign work and in foreign lives. I was spending each day with men and women who shared my experiences and feelings. I could see danger signs in myself. I stopped talking to my family about what was really happening. I hesitated in telling my husband about my new friendships. I wanted to ignore these behaviors as they were just too much to handle along with working and surviving each day. When my husband called, I seemed to have less to say to him than I did to the people I saw daily. I didn't know how to tell him what it was like to sit among warlords who had blood on their hands but still find a grain of respect for them. I heard General Dostum say, "I asked America for a few good men, and they sent me fighters with the hearts of lions and the courage of an army." Where did that come from in a man who was known as the butcher of the North? In everyone, I saw redemption.

And so, as it was for the big personalities in this conflict, so it was for me and many others. There was the stain of, for lack of a better word, sin on us all, but under it was the mark of redemption.

The work was clear. The needs were so great. It was like having everything marked in bold print for us. But our personal lives were more confusing. When I talked about it with others, in a very limited fashion, they explained how they accommodated the dichotomy of life away in a war zone. I knew some people had made peace with being two persons— the one on assignment and the one who went home. These people seemed to have found a way to separate who they were in both situations. I didn't think I could do that. I continued to struggle with how to be who I was becoming without losing who I had been when I left home. I was surprised at the conflict this created in me. I had enough trouble managing one life, never mind two. I wanted the comfort of being in my skin and knowing that who I was would work in Afghanistan and at home. I was confused about who, or what, was the real me.

One of the most confusing struggles of close living was the tight bonds that arose. And one of the mixed blessings of close living was the lack of privacy. It became a sort of built-in protection against misbehavior. There was neither time nor place for private intimacies, which were frowned on and against the military code of ethics. The embassy population was a cauldron of single and married people, young and old. This lack of privacy was an external control that helped prevent affairs from occurring. Like others, I got closer to and was attracted to some more than others. There was one marine who flirted with me and caught my attention. I was vulnerable to this attention. Given my marital commitment to Mike, I was grateful for the lack of opportunity to act on it. I often beat myself up for not feeling like I could, or would, ignore those feelings had there been a place of privacy. But there was not, and so I did not have an affair. When I look back, I now wonder why I would even be tempted, but then my aloneness, my stress, and my vulnerability were raw. I was facing so much in my everyday demands of work and survival that I had little reserves left for making good personal decisions.

I had to be strong when confronting the horrors surrounding me in Afghanistan. In the conflict, I had a hard time squaring how a whole group of people chose to live out what they interpreted as the call of God/Allah and at the same time inflict such pain on one another. I didn't want any part of that in my personal life, and this created a lot of stress in me. It was even more difficult than looking at hungry children. I needed support and a comforting presence. I needed someone to explain to me how an omnipresent, omnipotent god let this happen. I did not know how to talk about these thoughts. I was concerned that when I got home, there would be no words, no context, and no shared experiences to draw on to wade my way through this confusion. I was already carrying the load of previous assignments in Bosnia, Kosovo, Liberia, and elsewhere that should have been examined before jumping back into this morass of cruelty. I felt very alone in my confusion.

I had sought out a spiritual counselor in Washington when I returned from Kosovo the summer before 9/11. Her name was Charity, and she tried to get me to talk about the specifics of what I had seen and experienced during the Balkan war. She told me that God was in everything. I would not, could not, believe her. And I would not tell her my ugly stories. I felt like I would be contaminating a good and clean place in her life. In the end, I chose to carry the events, all of them, on my own. Now, here I was in Afghanistan, and they felt too heavy. Adding to the memories I carried from other lands and other people were the widows starving in their homes, the children withering away from the moment of their birth, and the butcher of the north, who ran over live prisoners with tanks to torment and kill them slowly. None of it made sense. How could I ask Charity to explain these events to me? How could I ask my family to walk through this dark tunnel with me? These questions weighed on me as I survived my days and nights in Kabul. When I looked at my fellow sojourners in this strange, magical, horrible, beautiful place, I wondered, *Am I one of them, or am I still part of my family and home in Washington?*

I did not know what to feel when I passed the sports stadium in the center of Kabul. It was built with expatriate money to provide a place for entertainment and sports. Under the Taliban, it was turned into an arena of death. It was the place where the Taliban took women on Sunday afternoons to publicly condemn them for their transgressions. Did she smile at a man she was not married to? Did she hold the hand of a lover? Did she dare to dream of choosing her own life path? Did she talk back to her husband? Did she refuse to accept another wife into her home? Did she dare to produce yet another baby girl? Where were the sons her husband demanded? In the end, it didn't matter what her transgression was—death was the sentence for her. None of them had a say in their ultimate fate. All were condemned to be stoned to death. *Ping. Ping. Ping.* If I listened hard enough, would I hear the landing of the stones? Should I look away in pain? Or should I look forward and hold my head up in respect and honor? So many women were taken to this sports stadium, dragged to the center field, and surrounded by angry, jeering men—their judges on the field and the spectators in the stands. Everyone was there to witness them being stoned to death on the bloodied ground. Some cheered the executioners. Some may have bowed their heads in shame. But no one stopped it. Everyone knew the cost of disobeying the Taliban. How long does it take to die from hundreds of stones pelting you?

I thought about all of this as I drove past the stadium, and I chided myself. *Who are you to fret about yourself? Who are you that you worry about the struggle in your life?* It was easy to dismiss the insignificant in the face of the overwhelming, and so all permission to take care of myself would vanish.

I came to Afghanistan to honor a promise to my son. Now I stayed to learn about life—mine and others. I stayed to work for those who had no justice or advocates in the sports stadium and for their families who must have loved them. My confusion around my life paled in comparison to theirs. Certainly, any transgressions in my life or those of my colleagues could not be measured on the same scale as stoning defenseless women to death.

I was plagued by these constant questions. For relief, I went out on the grounds of the embassy, sat, and laughed with colleagues with a glass of wine or a beer. It was everyone's way to escape for a few hours.

There was always another full day coming on the next day and the next and the next. I needed to stay focused on the task at hand. Maybe I would make it out better than the way I was when I had arrived. I knew I would have scars. One of my biggest questions was, did I need to hide those scars when I went home?

Chapter 21

Meetings in Kabul

The nights went by quickly in Kabul. I would drop into bed exhausted each night and fall into a deep, coma-like sleep. The sun rose early. I could feel it and know that it would be another scorching day in Afghanistan. And to add insult to injury, Afghanistan does not observe daylight saving time, so the sun rises in the summer between four thirty and five o'clock.

I was dreading this particular day. It was Sunday, the day of the big Afghan weekly humanitarian meeting held at the presidential palace, where the temporary government of Afghanistan was located. The area inside the gates was large and park-like, with sprawling lawns, sculptured rose gardens, and lovely trees. Trees were always a special luxury as they were not found in many areas of Kabul. Being on these lovely, well-tended, and secure grounds should have been a source of pleasure. But it was not.

The day's meeting was a routine weekly one with all of the humanitarian organizations and donors in attendance. The agenda was always to discuss existing humanitarian programs and planned humanitarian assistance for the next fiscal year. The donors—from other European countries, Japan, or Middle East Arab countries—and I, representing the US government, would give our updates on available money left in our budgets. I always dreaded being in this meeting with the Afghan government representative who headed up the humanitarian coordination for Afghanistan. He was a little man named Ashraf Ghani and reminded me of Mahatma Gandhi in looks; he was bald, wore an off-white shalwar kameez, and kept his head down, as though he was modest. However, this was not the case. He was cunning and always planning his next attack. I had heard he was sick with stomach cancer, so at first I felt sorry for him. But as the days and weeks passed, I lost all sympathy for him. He sat in meetings and nibbled on snacks in front of us, supposedly to alleviate stomach pain. I was told he needed to keep a small amount of food in his stomach at all times to prevent nausea. But in truth, he began to remind me of a rat nibbling on his stolen morsels. He was especially cruel. His manner of questioning anyone was to mock the person or organization. I knew he wanted to get his hands on the assistance money himself. He was sure he could do a better job of doling it out than any of the professionals sitting before him: foreign doctors, engineers, water sanitation specialists, nutritionists, and administrative managers who had traveled halfway around the world to be in the scorching heat of Kabul on this God-forsaken Sunday afternoon to help.

Sure enough, he was true to form in the meeting that day. I was trying to be as small as possible and hide in a back corner, but my stomach was churning. Ashraf found me, and I saw him grin.

"Mrs. McIntyre," he began with a sarcastic tone in his voice, "since we know that USAID thinks it can do whatever it wants to do in Afghanistan, would you be so kind as to tell us what those plans are?"

I replied with as much clarity and calm as I could. "Sir, I have submitted the plans for USAID disaster relief to your office as you requested. There is a spreadsheet of each activity presently being funded and thoughts on what we will fund next year." I knew he would rip into me. He seemed to hate the Americans even while he held dual passports—one for Afghanistan and one for the United States. He played out his own conflict on me that day.

"And you gave these supposed plans to whom? They are somewhere in my office, you say?"

"Yes, I gave the spreadsheets to your secretary, Mohammed. He said he would put them on your desk."

"Well, that is your word, but I have never seen them. Do you care to tell us what exactly the primary plans are before you go ahead and do things in Afghanistan without the permission of the government?" Nibble, nibble—crumbles of snacks went into his mouth.

"Of course. We will continue with the feeding programs for children under five years old, which is our primary health support in Kabul. We will also maintain our outreach both in Kabul and in the villages for clean water and shelter, as well as ongoing food support for families in need. And we will continue to fund the management of the Salang Tunnel—"

His head snapped up, his beady eyes bore into me from across the room, and he yelled, "You will *what*? This is why I don't want you doing things on your own! I have been in discussion with the World Bank to rebuild the Salang Tunnel. I don't want you wasting money on the tunnel when I have another donor to take care of it. This is the kind of coordination that you do not seem to understand, Mrs. McIntyre."

I felt small and belittled. I wanted to hide again like when I was a child and my father would yell at me. I stammered, "Sir, please, I do understand and—"

He again interrupted me and would not let me finish. It was a public embarrassment for me to be treated this way in front of forty or more of my professional colleagues. I never did get a chance to explain that I had already been in discussion with the World Bank. The plan was that the United States would fund only stopgap activities until the World Bank took over with real construction of the tunnel.

"Stop, I don't want to hear any more from you," he said. "I will talk to the ambassador myself and handle this appropriately." Turning to the people in the rest of the room, who sat in hushed discomfiture as he berated me, he said, "Please excuse me. I have to go to another meeting now." And he quickly exited the room.

This was not the first time he had done this to me. Once again, I was left sitting in silent humiliation as he insulted and belittled me in front of my colleagues. I hated it when he attacked and then, in his inimitable style, stood and left the meeting before a counterpoint could be made.

Others in the room had also felt his barbs, but he seemed to save the sharpest and most frequent for me. I was sick of him and his rudeness but had no recourse but to go back to the American embassy and explain yet another "scene" to my boss and the ambassador.

Week after week, this rude little man lashed out at me. I left each meeting shredded, angry, and on the verge of tears. I was mortified; I had come to Afghanistan to help, but he had done nothing but insult me. He was the epitome of Afghan male domination and disrespect.

Not all meetings were like those at the government house, thank goodness. Usually, I was able to speak and was listened to without interruption. Actually, USAID was a well-respected donor and the main one for humanitarian assistance. Most of the nongovernment organizations got funds from us to implement their assistance programs. As such, I was treated with respect.

At another routine weekly meeting in a UN office one afternoon, we were exchanging many good ideas: the NGO staff shared their findings from the villages where they worked, the UN offered its analysis of various crises, and other donor countries described their plans for the coming months. We charted the state of Afghanistan on a large map to identify and isolate gaps in services. Everyone was being collaborative and instructive. Then, suddenly, everyone got up and started to leave the room.

"What's happening?" I asked, surprised.

"Get your things and get out of the building," a colleague said.

Used to hearing emergency instructions, I did as I was told. It was not until I was standing that I felt it: an earthquake. I quickly became unsteady on my feet and disoriented. Up didn't quite feel like up, and standing straight was a challenge. I hurried to leave the building, climbing down the stairs from the third-floor meeting room while holding onto the railings. Once outside, I followed others to a clearing. It was my first time in an earthquake. The earth rolled. I felt like I was on a ship in the ocean, tottering and dizzy.

The shaking stopped after a few minutes, but still I was still shaking inside. I had never felt that way before. I immediately called my office in the embassy to see if they had felt it, too. They had. We could only wait and wonder what damage had been done and where the epicenter was.

I was struck by a parallel experience—I had just run from a shaking building at risk in Afghanistan, and my son had run from a building in New York City on 9/11. True, I ran down only three flights, while he had to get down eighty-nine. The thought of this parallel experience was like a punch in the stomach for me.

After a few hours, we began getting reports. The epicenter of the earthquake had been about one hundred miles north of Kabul and destroyed many homes. *Oh no, not this, too* was all I could think. Was there no end to the disasters and suffering in Afghanistan?

154

As more information came in, I learned that, true to form, the great NGOs working in the area of the earthquake had already started providing relief to the victims. What amazing young people these workers are.

And so this small earthquake marked another day in Afghanistan for me.

I never knew how each day would play out. The marines continued to ask me, "What's it like in Kabul?" I was usually at a loss as to what to tell them. They still told me how lucky I was to get out each day. I guess I was, but it was not always what I thought of as lucky.

Chapter 22

A Challenge: Working with the US Military

I met every week with the civil affairs units of the US military to coordinate the humanitarian assistance my office was offering and the work being done by the miltary. Each Saturday afternoon we sat in a bare, gray room with sparse furniture and echoing walls—and if we were lucky, a table to write on—to discuss the existing or upcoming programs. I had a list of our dozen of more funded humanitarian assistance partners, locations of activities, and what projects they were working on. In humanitarian circles, this is commonly called the three W's: who, what, and where. The five or six officers representing US Civil Affairs gave me a list of their ongoing projects and locations so that we could de-conflict any projects so we did not double-spend in one location. We all had projects in various stages of completion, and it was important that we knew who was still in what location. The de-confliction considered two concerns: first and the more practical was a look at what we were doing in our projects, and the second was consideration of the safety of the humanitarian teams when offensive military actions were planned in different locations. We did not want the humanitarian assistance workers to be caught in the middle of fighting. It was not unusual for me to be given a heads-up to stay out of a certain region for a certain amount of time. I never asked why; I just knew that there would be military activity there. I would notify my partners, as close as possible to any event, to come into Kabul for meetings for some real or fabricated reason to get them cleared of the area. The marines always took the lead on any military operations, and so the officers knew exactly where they wanted to be and what they wanted to accomplish. The US military had three primary goals: first, to achieve their military objectives; second, to fulfill civilian needs in any area they controlled; and third, to win the hearts and minds of the local population, especially the leaders. It was part of the military strategy to execute humanitarian activities within the areas of their operations and, by doing so, win over people who could assist them in military operations and knowledge.

There was always tension at these meetings, as the military would have liked to influence *my* programming to serve *their* goals. Military strategy of winning the hearts and minds was outside of my mandate, even though it was usually a positive spinoff of good humanitarian programming. I did not use humanitarian assistance to produce or reward good behavior, nor did I withhold humanitarian assistance to punish uncooperative behavior. Humanitarian programs and their recipients were decided on a needs-based-only process. While it was true that we did require assurance of staff safety, it is not part of international humanitarian assistance policy to ask which side of a war a village sat on, including this war. Humanitarian principles demand that we remain neutral, apolitical, and impartial in all our programs. This is our best hope for safety and protection. The expectation is that the people we work with will understand and trust that we are not part of the military machine. Keeping separation was imperative to all our operations. Since the US military was an active participant in this war and I represented the US government, it was even more important to maintain a separate identity. In this manner, we were more assured of securing our own safety and the safety of our partners. Our focus was based on who among the civilians needed assistance. We never provided any assistance to combatants from any side in a war zone.

This was certainly not a new concept for either the military or the humanitarians. During WWI and WWII, the military often provided assistance to the civilian populations in the areas they had captured. The International Federation of Red Cross and Red Crescent and the International Committee of Red Cross and Red Crescent societies always operated under the principles of impartiality, neutrality, and needs-based assistance. It was part of their code of conduct in providing services to noncombatants.

On one warm Saturday afternoon in Kabul, while sitting in the weekly meeting with my military friends, they expressed concern that some US assistance items had been found in enemy camps. This, of course, was of great concern to all of us and needed to be discussed at length. It was never our wish to aid and abet any military, and certainly not the enemies of our country.

"Listen, our troops are finding some of the food and medical supplies from the distributions up on the hillsides when we capture Taliban or Al Qaeda camps. It's obvious that the village people are sharing with the combatants in the nearby mountains," said one rather frustrated colonel.

"I am so sorry about this," I said. "But we need to bring the assistance in that area as the condition of the civilian population is very bad. My partners have done assessments and, quite frankly, the needs are greater there than in many of the surrounding villages. We cannot cut them out of aid."

"I said, the aid is getting up the hill to the enemy. You will have to do something about this!" the colonel exclaimed angrily.

"Again, I am sorry," I replied. "We are concerned about this, but we cannot overlook these women and children who are desperate for our help."

"Look, we all work for the same commander-in-chief, President Bush," he said. "As such, you will need to cease and desist your work in this area." Now the colonel was really getting upset. We all discussed how to best meet the needs of the civilians while not assisting the Taliban. Everyone offered options, but they were all rejected for one reason or another. It became obvious that we all had strong feelings about meeting our objectives but were at an impasse. We decided to put this topic on hold for a while and do some further problem-solving around the issue at a later date. I knew he could not stop me from taking assistance to those civilians in need, but I would see if anyone else, maybe one of our European country colleagues, could pick up this location. This was not a given since we were well into the year and the programs were already decided and money committed.

"I am so sorry," I said. "I certainly do not want any of our supplies to go to the enemy. Nor do I want any of our food or medical supplies to support even one terrorist who might pull a trigger on an American. But I am feeding the women and children in the villages. They are not combatants. As civilians, they have certain rights, even in war, to food, shelter, and basic medical care. How can we help meet my goals while we make sure we are not abetting any of the combatants?"

The colonel was angry.

"I do understand what you're saying, and I know that you're frustrated," I assured him, "but my job is to care for the civilians in need."

"There has to be a change," he said. "We cannot have our US military personnel battle for ground just to walk into a camp and find supplies marked 'Gifts from the American people.'" (This is a standard marking on humanitarian aid in most countries.) "I will take this back to Washington if we cannot come to a solution here."

I nodded. "We need to work together on this. Let's both think about it and reach back to our superiors in Washington for options that best serve both our causes."

Détente! It was a delicate situation.

He was not pleased with my response, but I could not change my job for him any more than he could change his job for me.

A week went by, and we met again. The atmosphere was cool, as we were all under pressure to do our jobs. I continued to plead my case: "You must also understand that the children and the women are as much victims in this war as the people in the Pentagon and World Trade Center were on 9/11. These women have no say in their personal lives, never mind in political activities. And certainly the children are innocent. They are suffering and hungry. Children are dying from simple infections for lack of medicine. Women die daily in childbirth for lack of care. I cannot terminate the assistance that is going to them."

Finally, there was a breakthrough. The suggestion was that the US troops, knowing that the villagers were supporting their men in the hills either by choice or under coercion, would monitor the hillsides to prevent the movement of supplies up to the enemy camps. We knew it might not always work, but it was a fair solution. And the fact was that we were not taking assistance to every place they were still actively fighting. Further, much of our assistance was screened for dual use, meaning items had limited use, such as children's medicines, baby food, women's medicine, maternity products, or female hygiene products that were not suitable for military personnel use. I agreed to give the colonel the list of distribution sites so he could use it to inform his men which areas needed to have extra patrols.

We ended in a stalemate but with a better understanding of the stresses for each of us. There are no perfect solutions in war, and we all knew that war was messy. Finding the right answers in the midst of conflicting agendas often involved a compromise.

I was disturbed to have such a disagreement between us when we were on the same side. I discussed it with my team when we met at the embassy, but we all agreed that humanitarian assistance could not be suspended or subject to the same rules as combat; innocent civilians needed to be taken care of. This was not something new. Civilians were never the targets in Afghanistan, but still were often victims. The stark reality is that any war machine embraces guns, bombs, terrorists, heroes, and soldiers. In the midst of those things sit the women, children, and elderly who need medicine, food, clean water, and shelter. This is the humanitarian assistance I was hired to address.

The colonel and I agreed to work together. I would continue to feed the women and children, and the soldiers would continue to fight the battles. And we would remember that we were on the same side.

We worked hard to maintain and improve relations over the next few weeks. Many of the officers understood, but personalities come into relationships even in war, and one of the officers remained really angry that he could not give me a direct order as he did his troops. This would be a sticking point that we faced in the days and months to come. It was a challenging relationship at best, and one that found its way into every war zone.

Humanitarian workers are not under the command of any military in any war zone—even when the military is the United States Armed Forces.

Chapter 23

Personal Visit with a General

I had an opportunity to engage with our American military there again after a long day on the road visiting sites of humanitarian assistance. This one was of a decidedly different nature and more personal.

The rough wooden sign arched over the dirt road said, "Bagram Air Force Base." I had not been on the base before but wanted to connect with someone there at the request of family back home. Since we were driving by and had time in our schedule, I decided to ask my driver to turn in. I always traveled with my American diplomatic passport and thought I could use that and my American embassy ID as credentials to gain entrance. I thought, *what's the worst that can happen—they will turn us away?* Plus, our vehicle had American embassy markings. I instructed Abdulaman, my driver that day, to turn left onto the road leading into the base. He did so with great trepidation. I'm sure he was worried that he would be held at gunpoint and maybe interrogated. He was probably afraid that he would be shot. I tried to soothe his fears by saying that, in this case, I would do all the talking—a juxtaposition to our usual agendas. This was of little comfort to him, I could tell from the quick sneer that crossed his face. I knew he doubted my words, given the fact that I was a woman and was asking him to enter the belly of the beast of American military might in Afghanistan. But I was on a personal mission, a rarity for me in Afghanistan.

A dozen or so soldiers were standing guard at a makeshift, rusted, four-inch-diameter hinged pipe that served as a barrier. Immediately they became alert as our car drove slowly toward them. They pointed rifles at us, shouting for us to stop. Abdulaman hit the brakes and, in a cloud of dust, we screeched to a stop. I wasn't prepared for such a sharp response and banged against the back of the front seat.

"What are you doing?" I exclaimed. "Tell me the next time you're going to stop like that."

Abdulaman only groaned back at me, "Guns, madam."

"Yes, I see them, but they won't shoot if you follow instructions and let me do the talking." I rolled down the back window and shouted out rather pleasantly, "I'm an American! Can I get out of the car?"

"What?" called back one of the soldiers. "Do not approach!"

Okay, so now we're shouting. "I'm an American from the American embassy! Can I get out of the car?" I shouted back, more loudly while trying to still be pleasant.

"Everyone get out of the car. Keep your hands were we can see them," another soldier said.

Abdulaman complied immediately, hands in the air. He was shaking. I opened my back door, again identifying myself as an American, and stepped out with my hands held forward, if not exactly up in surrender. We watched as the solders approached carefully. At this time there had been no suicide attacks on our soldiers, but they were trained to expect anything.

They were surprised to see me climb out, an American civilian woman in a brightly colored shalwar kameez and smiling at them.

"Who are you? What are you doing here?" questioned the closest soldier, not shouting now.

"I'm Sue McIntyre from the American embassy, and I'd like to see General McNeill."

"Can we see some ID?" he asked.

"Yes, of course. It is in my backpack in the car. May I get it? I have two things, my American diplomatic passport and my embassy ID badge."

The soldier let me reach into the back seat and get my backpack out. I dug in, found my IDs, and presented them to him. Seemingly satisfied, although still surprised, he said I could enter. Abdulaman was stunned. The soldier turned to him and said he needed to search him. He complied. I told them he was my driver, been cleared by security at the embassy, and was allowed to come and go from the embassy. He also had a badge, which he showed to them. We were told we could drive forward to the next barrier, where the car would again be stopped.

We got back in the car and proceeded very slowly. Abdulaman may have been ready to pee his pants at this point. I was finally among my own countrymen. There was a comfort in knowing I was surrounded by Americans, if only here in this small camp of soldiers outside of Heaven. The embassy was home for me but isolated. This felt more like the soil and land of Afghanistan, and here were American soldiers speaking English to me. Lovely!

When we drove to the next barrier about a quarter of a mile down the dirt road, we stopped again. These men were not surprised to see us, as the soldiers at the outside gate had radioed them to notify them of our approach.

I was permitted out of the car, and they reviewed my documents again. I was told that I could proceed on foot, but Abdulaman and the car would have to stay at this checkpoint. I turned to Abdulaman and told him to just sit tight and do nothing, and I would be back. A soldier was assigned to guard him as I turned to walk another quarter of a mile or so toward the tents where I had been directed.

At this time, Bagram Air Base was little more than a collection of tents clustered together beneath the rocky crags of mountains. The field held a scattering of various-size aircraft parked on a rather poorly defined runway. The surrounding perimeter was constructed of wooden fence posts and barbed wire. *Not a very intimidating fence*, I thought. I reminded myself that this had once been a Soviet air base. The conditions were very poor, and there did not appear to be any permanent structures around. I wondered if this was how the Soviet military lived for their ten years of occupation in Afghanistan. It was pretty rough.

I continued to ask directions to the general's location from men that I passed. I was ushered forward and pointed to a larger tent. I went straight to it and was met at the outer flap by another soldier. "Ma'am, can I help you?" asked the soldier.

"Yes, is this General McNeill's tent?"

"Yes, ma'am, but do you have an appointment with him?" he asked doubtfully. After all, a drop-in visit to the general could not have been common, to say the least.

"No, I was just driving by and wanted to stop in to see him," I said. Now he looked at me with real skepticism. "Really," I said. "I'm working at the American embassy in Kabul and was on my way home when I saw the sign for Bagram Air Base. I thought I might find General McNeill here." He asked me to wait as he stepped inside for a moment. I could hear muffled talk, and then he came out with another soldier of higher rank. He was a major, and he assumed responsibility for me at this point.

"Step in from the heat, ma'am, and let's talk about why you are here."

Getting out of the sun was such a relief. It had taken me about thirty minutes to get to this point. I thanked the major and entered the tent. I was in a sort of anteroom with a canvas wall between me and the next chamber. I again explained that I had been driving by and wanted to see the general.

"What is the nature of your business with the general?" the major asked.

"Well, actually, it's personal," I responded. This got a look of surprise. I cringed at how that might have sounded, but the major did a snappy turn and walked behind the interior curtain. Again I heard muffled talking. It was a bit longer this time before the major opened the canvas divider and called me in. Finally, there was General McNeill, sitting behind a rather plain wooden table serving as his desk. All the papers had been turned over so as not to expose any work to me. He looked at me with curiosity and not a little confusion.

"Hello," I said cheerily. "I'm Sue McIntyre from the American embassy." I had learned that noting the American embassy was like having a gold card: it opened all doors.

"Hello, and how can I be of assistance today?" General McNeill replied rather formally. I was suddenly aware that this was not playing out the way I had imagined. I ran some pertinent data through my brain and realized that this was not an ordinary call on a North Carolina homeboy. This was the commanding general of the American armed forces in Afghanistan. Boy, had I jumped into this one without a lot of thought.

"Sir, this is rather unusual, but I really just stopped by to say hello and bring greetings from Dick and Linda Lewis in Fayetteville. Linda mentioned that she was a good friend of your wife and said that if I saw you I should give you her best regards. She is my daughter's mother-in-law. So when I was driving by on the road and saw the sign for Bagram, I thought

I would check to see if you were here. I know that you're real busy, so I won't keep you," I said, backing away as my voice petered out.

"Just what are you doing here?" he asked. "I mean here in Afghanistan."

I explained my job and said that I had been here since the winter, working and coordinating with the military in Kabul. He asked me to sit and had a number of questions, and asked for clarification of my connection to the Lewises in Fayetteville. Finally, we were on the same page and started to get along quite nicely. I knew this visit had come at him out of the blue, and it took a minute for him to catch up with me. He offered me tea or coffee. I declined and thanked him for giving me his time. He told me he couldn't turn me away without finding out who I was and what I was doing there since I'd said my visit was personal.

"'Personal' was the last thing I expected here in Afghanistan," he said with a grin. I was relieved that he had a good sense of humor about my dropping in. I thanked him again, offered to assist him in any I could with my humanitarian programs, and said goodbye.

I walked back out into the heat of the day, marveling at what I had just done. I thought, *Wait till I tell my daughter that I found her in-laws' friend in Afghanistan and actually stopped in to see him, the commander of our forces here. Holy shit, was I hot!*

I found Abdulaman waiting impatiently for me. He was still nervous and jumped back in the car to get us out of there as quickly as he could. What a story he would have to tell to his friends when he got safely home that night, "Inshalla!"

Chapter 24

Shopping on Chicken Street

Not all my forays into Kabul, or Afghanistan, were work related. After a number of weeks there I learned of an interesting street in the center of Kabul. It was called Chicken Street. Chicken Street was the main shopping district at the time I was in Kabul. Small, eclectic shops lined the street. Like Flower Street, another commercial street downtown, Chicken Street was the official name of this Fifth Avenue of Kabul. I never did find out why. I assumed it was because chickens were sold there at some point, but when I was there, chickens were about the only thing *not* sold in this exotic flea market. Maybe the name was a throwback to better times in Kabul when markets were full and commerce flourished.

Shopping was a social event. We usually went in twos or threes from the embassy, never a larger group, which would have attracted too much attention. Our outings involved getting an embassy car reserved for our time off and heading to town with money in hand, preferably dollars. No one particularly wanted the local currency, which was unstable and fluctuated from week to week. It was fascinating to walk around and see the goods ranging from trash to treasures, from the commonplace to the most exotic.

In the first months after our entry into Kabul, the very sight of an American woman strolling down the street was enough to create a stir among the locals. Within a few months, I was used to being stared at. I didn't fit in and never would unless I wore a burqa, which we had been instructed by the embassy's security detail not to do. Our very anonymity could be cause for injury if we were to unknowingly break a rule. The practice in Kabul during Taliban days, and still in effect, was that any man could beat any woman who was immodest or alone. If I was covered, no man would know that I was a foreigner, and I might have been caned before I could alert them that I was not one of their women. So while I never wore a burqa, I did wear the shalwar kameez and a hijab to respect the norms of that culture. In this attire, my face always showed, and I could easily be distinguished as a foreigner.

This day I was wearing a bright red-and-white patterned shalwar kameez. I already stood out, so I decided to indulge my preference for color and go for it. My head was appropriately covered with a shawl, which was forever slipping backward and revealing my blonde hair.

Two female friends from the embassy and I were besieged by hawkers selling their wares from the various shops. They knew we had money to spend and dangled goods in front of our eyes. We were both politely and not so politely accosted depending on the desperation of the shop owner. On this day, a very unusual item was presented to me: a beautiful leopard-skin coat.

"This be perfect for madam," the shopkeeper told me in broken English. "You buy this and be beautiful on you."

"How old is this?" I asked.

"Very big treasure of fifty or more years," the merchant replied.

How could I resist this? I was adamantly against the killing of endangered animals for clothing, but this was a real piece of vintage clothing. What to do?

"I will think about it. How much is it?"

"For you? Only five hundred US dollars."

"No, that is way too much," I said. "If I decide to buy it, I will give you one hundred."

The haggling began. This was how it worked for any purchase. The price was never fixed until both parties agreed on it. I knew a new offer was coming.

"You kill me. I give it to you for three hundred," the merchant said.

"No, my best offer is one hundred and fifty," I said and began to turn away.

He snapped out, "Okay, last price two hundred, but only for you."

"Okay, but I am still going to think about it at that price since it will be a souvenir only," I said. "I really don't think I can wear it back home."

I could tell he was perplexed as to why I would buy a coat and then not wear it, but I guess he put it down to the strangeness of American women. He just could not imagine buying a coat while planning on not wearing it. I explained that I was against killing endangered animals, but this wasn't an issue for him. All life was endangered for everyone in Afghanistan. Why would it be any different for the leopard?

I understood. I had been there long enough to know that people struggled enough to keep their families alive, never mind wild animals.

I then moved on down the street to one of the many carpet shops. Here, I was faced with yet another decision of conscience. I knew that the women and children who made the carpets were not paid directly for their beautiful, labor-intensive work. Should I buy or not? It was always the question. I was told that the men made a living for their families selling the carpets, and so, by extension, the women and children were paid in food and clothes for their work. I decided not to buy a carpet on that day but enjoyed looking at the amazing, deep red carpets with black-and-gray-patterned circles so familiar in Kabul. The carpets were usually of thick wool yarn and ranged in size from two by three feet to ten by twelve feet. The large carpets were very heavy. But in spite of this, the shopkeepers tugged one after another off the shelves in hopes of making a sale. They would shake them out and offer them for viewing, producing a lot of dirt and dust flying about. I quickly learned to turn my face away during this process. There was no end to the seller's energy as carpet after carpet was pulled from the shelf and laid out on the dirt floor of the shop one on top of another. It was always a trick to get out of a shop without making a purchase. The disappointed shopkeeper would look at me like I was personally denying him his livelihood.

In another shop, I saw a beautiful translucent blue vase in the window. "It is from Herat," the owner said as I gazed at it. I hadn't gotten to visit Herat yet. It was located on the very western border of Afghanistan next to Iran. I was fascinated by this city, which was reported to have large boulevards with trees down the centers. It was also a city under the iron hand of General Mohammed Ismail Khan, a Tajik warlord who was known as the Lion of Herat. He was a local hero, much like General Massoud, the Lion of Panjshir, was in the northeast. The Afghans are a poetic people at heart, and their local nicknames often reflect that trait.

The dark cerulean blue vase sitting on the shelf before me was lovely in its simplicity. It may have been a throwback to earlier Persian times, which still heavily influenced the western regions of Afghanistan. The shared border with Iran was porous, and much of the culture there could find its roots in Persian art rather than the Oriental influence in the eastern regions separated from the west by vast mountain ranges and beautiful, fertile valleys. This vase was like no other I had seen locally. I was intrigued and quite interested in buying it. I usually don't buy glassware, as it is a pain in the neck to pack and carry home safely. But this one called to me.

"It's beautiful. How much is it and how old is it?" I asked, trying to sound nonchalant. I didn't want to give the game away from the first get-go. I turned to look at other items as I waited for the shopkeeper's reply.

"It is fifty dollars US," he said. "I would guess it to be at least one hundred years old, as the glass is made in a primitive style. Look, see how it reflects the light through its imperfections?"

I turned to look and was quite impressed. But still I gasped, "Are you kidding me? I cannot pay that much for something that might not even make it home in my suitcase. I'll give you ten dollars."

It was his turn to look aghast. And so again, the negotiations started. Haggling was part of the process, and any good merchant relished the play. "No, no! You are stealing it from me." Such dramatics.

"All right, I'll give you twenty dollars." Shock, response, counteroffer— and so it went for about twenty minutes. After this back-and-forth dance, with the dollar amount reducing in smaller and smaller increments, we settled on thirty dollars. He was happy since he had come out on the top half of the original price, and I was happy to be buying this stunning original handmade vase.

As I left the shop, I could see in the daylight that the vase was a deep blue like the Greek blues of the Mediterranean. It was lovely with its handmade flaws refracting light in uneven and interesting ways. I was unsure if I could get it home unbroken, but for the agreed-upon price it was worth the gamble.

Later, on another day of shopping, I found another beautiful vase painted with gold leaf and in a design unique to the eastern, more Oriental regions of Afghanistan. It was carved of wood and had a much better chance of safely surviving my trip home. Both were treasures I would enjoy having.

⌒⋎⌒

Shopping expeditions to Chicken Street usually entailed me encountering three little girls who must have lived nearby. They looked to be between eight and ten years old and went about their day's work of begging. They often escorted me from shop to shop, and I paid them to carry bags for me. This was something I would never had done with boys for fear they would have run away with my parcels, but something told me the girls would not do this and would like the experience of shopping with me. I particularly liked these three girls, whom I got to know. Unfortunately, the communication was stilted, given language barriers, but we managed. The girls were lovely and, with time, they became a bit bolder. Their curiosity to touch me and talk with me in halting English began to emerge. Smiles, understood in all languages, went a long way. Soon the girls, in their floppy, ill-fitting shoes, tap-tapped along behind me on a regular basis. I learned their names—Rashida, Zahra, and Hawa. They all had long, dark brown hair and were slim but not skinny. Their clothes were poor, but not as dirty as some I had seen who begged in the streets. Zahra had the beautiful, haunting, deep green eyes found in Afghanistan. Rashida was the boldest of the three and seemed to be the leader. Maybe she was the oldest. It was hard to tell about exact age because of the limited food, which resulted in girls particularly being small. But Hawa became my favorite. She had a ready smile and was quick to catch on to my pantomimed meanings. She had the sharp eyes of a keen intellect, and I wished so much that that very intelligence would not be wasted in this restrictive culture that limited the possibilities for girls.

Each was anxious to see what I would buy. Shopkeepers often shooed them away, but I always interceded on their behalf. I let the shopkeepers know that the girls were with me. They were my advisors of sort. They would frown when the price was too high and nod if the price was good. They were my inside-trader consultants. Of course, they knew that at the end of my shopping spree I would give each of them a few Afghanis to take home for their families. But I also hoped I provided them with an image of women previously unseen in their culture, who could shop independently, spend her own money, and travel from a foreign land to work without a man over her. I hoped that this knowledge would stay with them as they grew. I wanted them to be aware that there were alternative ways for women to live other than that demanded of them in Afghanistan.

In the end, I did buy the leopard coat, though I never expected to wear it. I enjoy looking at it as a treasure from a time and place long before I knew of Kabul when hunting outings were plentiful. It might disturb some people, but it was my choice to own this rare thing of beauty.

Chapter 25

Legs for Sale and Sniffer Dogs

I arranged a treat for the American ambassador, the USAID mission director, and some of my team. I had requested an invitation from the Norwegian Mine Action Committee team to visit their dog-training school. I'd heard that it was an amazing place. We got into our cars and drove outside of the protective gates of Heaven by seven in the morning. Since it was early in the day, the normal traffic of Kabul prevailed. Horns honked. Afghan traffic cops in black trousers and white uniform shirts stood, at great peril, in the middle of the streets trying to direct traffic. It was always chaotic in morning traffic, with cars that were trying to hurry through intersections and ended up stuck facing each other in a game of chicken. Who would move first? There wasn't one car that was worth much. Banged-up Toyota pickups twenty years old or more, old Soviet Lada sedans, and even an occasional old Ford or two could be spotted stuck in the traffic jam. These vintage vehicles were invariably rusty, dirty, dented, and piled high with men off to work or to the market. There might be a few chauffeur-driven cars from wealthier families, indistinguishable from others except for a woman who would be seated in the back being driven someplace. The streets were crowded with all means of transportation. It was not surprising to see donkey-drawn carts and horses with half a family seated on top. Added to the mix were the men on foot. This group demanded their space on roads as well as sidewalks. They were not to be ignored given their large numbers.

I was struck by one man in the midst of all this chaos. "What is that man doing on the side of the road?" I asked. "Does he need help?"

Jamal had come to expect anything from me over the months of being my driver. Without batting an eye, he did a quick look to see what I was asking about. He said, "He is selling his leg."

"What? Why?" I was stunned. Again, I was hit by the notion that what was normal to Afghans was amazing to me. I thought, *How can my driver be so laissez-faire about this?* The hard realities of life in a country at war for thirty years made people desperate beyond my imagination. I was often shocked by unexpected scenes, as I was on that morning. This was daily life in Afghanistan. I wanted to talk more about it.

"Tell me what is happening, please," I said to Jamal.

"When money is needed and there is no other means to get it, many amputees will sell their prosthetic legs in order to help the family. It is often the only means, as cripples, for them to help support their families. It is a way for them to bring in money."

And I wondered, in that hustling, dusty market, did someone stop in their daily shopping, notice this man, and think, *Ah, I have been looking for a leg. Let me get this one for my brother who lost his!* It seemed so improbable. Yet there was the man, selling his leg.

"If he sells it, what will he do to get around?"

Jamal smiled patiently at my confusion. Apparently it was quite obvious to him. "He will take the money home. He will then hop around on his crutches until he can get another leg from yet another NGO making them."

Elementary commerce, explained in the most practical of terms. There was a market for legs, and as in any economy, supply and demand dictated the market. The need for legs in Afghanistan was high. I guessed prosthetic legs were like a third-world shoe—a close fit seemed to be good enough. This was certainly contrary to the perfect fit demanded in the rest of the world, especially for prosthetics.

The high demand for prosthetic legs was a result of the land-mine-riddled countryside. They were left over from years of war with the Soviet Union, as well as the thousands more added during the civil war that followed. Mines are the number-one crippler of children in Afghanistan.

Our team was providing public education about land mines with posters displaying pictures of them. These were hung at clinics, in government buildings, and even in shops if the owners were willing. We provided funding to our NGO partners to support local teachers with materials to include land-mine awareness in school for their students.

I imagined how I might feel sending my children off to school where they had to learn about land mines.

In an effort to expand our knowledge about this ominous threat to all Afghans and to better understand what more might be done to alleviate civilian injuries, we were meeting with the Norwegian Mine Action Committee removal team, which, along with physically removing land mines, had started a school to train dogs to sniff out bombs and mines.

The school was about a forty-five-minute drive from the embassy. Since the trip included the ambassador, we traveled from the embassy compound in armored vehicles.

At the training site, we came upon a well-cared-for wire-fenced enclosure set in a secluded area. We were met by the director from the Norwegian Mine Action Committee, who ran the training school. The physical complex consisted of a number of pale green metal sheds set on a small incline. It included classrooms for human trainers and handlers as well as outdoor classrooms for the dogs, who looked to be primarily German shepherds. The grades were kindergarten through fourth grade for the dogs. There were about a dozen dogs in the early classrooms and five or six in the advanced classrooms. As the training became more advanced, some dogs were not smart enough to be trained in this critical work and were dropped from the program.

Our tour began inside, where we were briefed by the Norwegian staff and watched a training film for the staff. I was quite pleased to see that the ambassador and the USAID mission director immediately became deeply engaged. I'd worked hard to get the outing organized. It was not easy to carve out an entire morning for something with two such important, busy people. My goal was to support and encourage international funding for this vital training program.

The truly amazing thing about this program was that the cost-benefit ratio was, without question, convincing. How could you equate the cost of training a dog against the value of a child's life or limb? You couldn't.

After the film, we headed outside where the real action was taking place. The pups were like all puppies, with lots of energy and very short attention spans. They tumbled and played and barked with glee. Everyone fell in love with one cutie after another. After a few minutes in this classroom, we moved on to the first graders. Already there was a difference. These pups were more attentive and had a fixed daily schedule. They were given plenty of playtime, but when in training, they became more serious. And so it went until we reached the fourth graders. They displayed the marked discipline of well-trained working dogs. They were not to be spoken to or distracted when on the job. It usually took the entire four years to train a dog to be proficient in bomb sniffing—hence the grades one through four.

We were amazed at the focus and discipline of these remarkable dogs. The team gave us a demonstration of the training exercises for each level but took special pride in bringing a few of the "graduates" out to show us their skills. The training course had a run with buried explosives, which the dogs had to find each morning. The explosives were relocated every night, making each morning a new challenge. Car explosives were also hidden in vehicles around the compound, and the dogs were on alert to search and find them. The dogs were also trained to protect their handlers by blocking a pathway that led to a buried explosive device.

Watching the clearing of a land-mined field was so highly stressful that we became exhausted in a matter of minutes. The tension was palpable. It reminded me of a child's jack-in-the-box toy, when one turns the handle slowly, anticipating the moment of the expected *pop*. We all felt the tension as the men and dogs inched forward a millimeter at a time, using tiny metal probes to meticulously feel for mines. The sniffer dogs worked diligently along with the men. The work was painstakingly slow. The team moved across the field until they pronounced it cleared.

We were all very impressed, in awe of both the dogs and the trainers. This job took years of patient and skilled preparation. The cost was daunting, but again, we came back to the question—what is the value of a life or limb saved?

The morning was a great success. I knew that when I next recommended funding a mine-awareness and dog-training program, I would have important allies in the ambassador and the mission director.

When we returned to the American embassy, we looked at our own sniffer dogs and handlers with new appreciation. We entered the embassy gates; passed the "Guns of Navarone," as I had dubbed our welcoming machine guns pointing outward at the entrance; and swung the vehicle sharply to the right into a dead zone, which was a field situated away from other personnel and the embassy building. In this sandy patch of ground, our sniffer dogs went into action. We sat patiently as they circled the car, looking for explosives.

Chapter 26

The Wedding

I was going to a wedding in Afghanistan.

One of my Afghan staff members, Miriam, invited me to her sister's wedding. I was excited, though I couldn't help reminding myself that we were at war. I became aware that even in war, life went on. That included weddings, births, deaths, laundry, housekeeping, and preparing dinner. The mundane comingled with the unthinkable on a daily basis.

Getting ready for a wedding presented many of the same questions I would have back home. What should I wear? I really had no idea, but luckily for me, I had only a few choices—not including the black fishnet dress. I chose what I considered my best option, a light pink, patterned cotton shalwar kameez with a matching head scarf.

I didn't know what I should bring as a gift. I enlisted the help of the Afghan staff for ideas. There were many suggestions, all available in the local markets. In the end, however, I decided that a gift of money was the most practical and the most needed. Dollars were always preferred, making this an easy last-minute choice for me.

I was excited about my first foray into Kabul social life. I fixed my hair and put on makeup. I didn't want to insult the family by showing up looking too casual. As the mother of one of my girlfriends in New York used to say, "One can never be overdressed." I was counting on that principle. This was the most care I had taken with my appearance in a long time. I wanted to enjoy myself as it was a celebration in the midst of so much suffering, a touch of ordinary life in the middle of a war zone. Having a wedding in Afghanistan symbolized hope.

I signed out of the embassy compound with another colleague who was also invited and arranged for my driver, the ever-faithful Jamal. I picked up a handheld radio as required when going off the embassy compound—not the normal accessory for wedding attire. I also had my new cell phone from a new business that had opened in Kabul. I fit it all into my rather large handbag that looked a bit like a small backpack, but it was the best I could do.

Jamal and Jonathan, my colleague, and I drove off. I began asking Jamal, my well-used human Afghan encyclopedia, for information on what to expect at the wedding. "How should I behave?" was my first question.

Jamal had loosened up over the months and now showed more of his personality, which included a wicked sense of humor. "Act like a nice lady," he said with a grin.

"Nice for whom, Americans or Afghans?" was my quick reply. Two could play this game.

"A nice woman to please Allah," he said.

"Okay, but how does a good woman of Allah behave at an Afghan wedding?"

"You will be separated from Jonathan when you enter. He will go with the men, and you will be taken to the women's side of the curtain. On that side you will be seated at a table with other women. Then just follow what they do." This was long-winded for Jamal, who was usually a man of few words.

Jonathan asked a few questions. "As a male guest not related to either side of the family, are there restrictions on where I can go within the hall and with whom I may speak?"

"You will be okay if you just stay on the men's side of the curtain and only talk to men," replied Jamal.

"Seems simple enough," Jonathan said.

"Okay, I'll stay with the women, and you'll stay with the men. But let's set a time to leave or a way to communicate if necessary," I said, ever the planner that I'd become in Kabul. "We can use our cell phones if possible, or if worse comes to worst, call me on my handheld radio."

"Damn, I didn't bring a handheld since you had yours. I didn't think I needed one," Jonathan admitted with some chagrin.

"Well, now I'm stuck carrying this big thing and you got away without it," I said. "We'll have to make sure our cell phones work before going into the wedding hall. If not, let's all agree on a set time to leave." I was angry that he hadn't carried his radio with him. This was an important safety protocol. Besides the inconvenience that I had with this rather bulky radio, he was out of compliance.

"Okay, Jamal, a few more questions," I said. "Is there a special table or someone that I should give my gift card to? It does have some money in it for the bride, so I don't want it to get lost."

"Sue, you are so worried about everything. Just go in and if you do not see a table for gifts, just give the card to the bride," Jamal said. He was getting a bit tired of my endless questions. I decided not to ask him if I was dressed appropriately as it was too late to change anyway. I was curious as to how the other ladies would be dressed but knew I would see for myself soon enough. And these queries might have been of a bit too personal nature and cause him embarrassment.

But I couldn't help myself asking just a few more. "Is it an arranged marriage? Do you think the bride knows the groom? Will I see the groom?" I was so curious. Weddings are universal but some elements are very particular to each society. If Jamal couldn't answer me, I could ask Miriam more questions next week when we returned to work. I hadn't thought about so many issues when Miriam had invited me on Thursday to attend the wedding on Saturday. Such was the way life here: short notice even for major events.

We soon arrived at the wedding hall at the end of a yet another dirt road on the outskirts of Kabul. Wedding halls are traditional in Afghanistan, as in many Middle Eastern countries. The parking area around the hall was filled with vehicles of all kinds and makes. There were the standard "best of the family" cars for the bride and bridal party. There were the normal relatives' cars and also military vehicles—armored cars, small tanks, and a few large transport trucks, which added a new dimension to the wedding experience for me. We had a hard time finding a good place to park the big embassy car. I did not want Jamal to be blocked in should we need to leave in a hurry. I also wanted to be able to leave before the other guests. Many of the local wedding celebrations could go on for hours, and I knew we could not stay that long. Jamal got out and spoke to some men standing in the entrance. I guess they came to an agreement to allow Jamal to park just to the side of the steps going into the hall. We managed to squeeze between a military jeep of indeterminate age and a large transport truck. I was adamant that he stay right there. I did not want to have to look for him when we were ready to leave, especially if there was an emergency and we were forced to leave in a hurry. He promised to stay put. I was always clear that the driver's responsibility was to protect the vehicle, and as such, he knew his job depended on his remaining beside the car.

The rented hall was a large building designed expressly to host weddings. It was two stories high and made of gray cinder blocks. There was no landscaping, just the ever-present dirt and dust of Kabul in the summertime.

Jonathan and I stepped out into the dirt. I tiptoed my way around puddles and over rocks. As soon as we entered the door, I was quickly ushered to the left and up a set of stairs to a private room. Jonathan was pulled to the right, and that was the last I saw of him before getting back in the car to return to the embassy.

As I entered a private room on the second floor, I thought it looked like a bridal dressing area, similar to what we might find back in the States. It was full of chattering women wearing the most amazing assortment of colors—no soft pastel palate for these women, who may have been the bridesmaids. I saw bright orange, red, yellow, lime green, peacock green, dazzling silver and gold, and vivid blue in shimmery satins and taffeta fabrics. It took me a minute to acclimate to the sudden riot of color after so many months of brown and gray and the ubiquitous light blue burqas. Stunned, I stood still for a moment. I was also immediately aware of the dull picture I made in my pale-pink cotton outfit that suddenly looked like pajamas to me. Stiletto heels and hair piled high on their heads made all the ladies look tall. And to top it all off, they were splashed with glitter—on their faces, their expansively exposed cleavage, their shoulders, and their arms and backs. It was even in their teased hair. Boy, was I underdressed!

I wondered if I was in the wrong place. Why was I in the bridal room with intimate family members? Again, I found myself in unfamiliar waters and somehow always in the deep end of the pool. Jamal had not told me about this. Maybe, being a man, he didn'tt know about this secret chamber of rainbow-colored women glittering as if from a Broadway show. I fell back on my standard behavior—smile and greet them all with a gracious "Salam Alakum?"

The chatter stopped, and all the kohl-lined eyes looked at me. I was becoming uncomfortable. They stared at me and then, miracle of miracles, one of the older women came to me and spoke English. I was so relieved.

"Who are you?" she asked in the softest of voices, neither unkind nor threatening.

"I'm Sue, Miriam's coworker from the American embassy," I answered, hoping I had been expected. "Where is Miriam?"

"She is here, but she just left the room for a moment."

"Thank you," I said. "I think I'm in the wrong place right now. The greeter at the door ushered me up here when I came in. Where should I go?"

"No, we are honored to have you here," the woman replied. "You are welcome to stay with us until we go downstairs for the reception." This was true Afghan hospitality. They would have never made me feel unwelcome. Again I was surprised at the graciousness of Afghan women. "Please sit over here by my nieces."

I sat. It gave me a moment to observe more closely the goings-on until finally Miriam came in. I was so grateful to see her. She immediately spied me, the washed-out one in this room full of vibrantly painted women.

"Welcome, Sue. I am so glad you came!" she exclaimed affectionately.

"I am so sorry that I'm not dressed appropriately," I apologized. "You know I have so little here, and this is the best dress I have."

"You look fine," she said. I knew this was not true. The others were quite a startling contrast in their long, formal dresses with low-cut bodices. I was still in shock. I hadn't seen that much flesh since exiting my shower that morning. Not to belabor the point, but the room was full of overflowing bosoms and high-rising leg slits on the sides of the dresses. It looked like a cheaper version of the red carpet at the Oscars. I was very village-vintage in my plain clothes, definitely underdressed.

Pulling my focus away from all the sparkling flesh, I again focused on their makeup and hair, thinking that it could rival anything one might see in a Las Vegas show. Their makeup was heavy, accentuating their beautiful dark eyes. Their uncovered hair was finally free to cascade down their backs or be piled to new heights on their heads. Color had been sprayed in their hair to match the color of their garments, then layered over with a touch of glitter for extra accent. My hair was neither long nor glorious, nor did it match my dress. I was a dismal spirit standing in the neon marvel of these glorious Afghan women.

"Please have some tea and cookies while we wait to go downstairs," the English-speaking older woman said. I had learned that she was Miriam's aunt, a former schoolteacher in the Soviet days when women were freer to work and travel on their own.

Since I had no clue as to what was going on, I just sat, drank my tea, and feasted my eyes. I had no idea what they were all saying, and my only contribution was a polite Pashtu thank you, "*Tashakor,*" for the proffered refreshments.

I was shocked when a man came into the room. Miriam whispered quickly to me, "It's the groom." When he went to sit next to one of the brightly dressed girls, I assumed it was his new bride, as this detail had not been apparent to me before.

"He is related to all the women in the room and with his wife now, so that is why he is allowed in," explained Miriam's aunt. "We will take some photos now. You must be in them."

"Oh no, I'm not properly dressed and I'm not family," I pleaded but to no avail. Apparently it was of no concern that I was not a relative. I was scooped up and placed in the photos, front and center next to the bride!

I smiled for the photos, but then I noticed that no one else was smiling. I was so confused. I made a mental note to ask Miriam about it later.

After multiple photos, all with me smack in the middle grinning like the family idiot, I was told that we were to head down to the reception hall. The guests had all arrived and been appropriately seated.

As we entered the large room, I understood why we had been held back. The men were all seated on one side of the hall and the women on the other, with a floor-to-ceiling sliding curtain between us, effectively separating the space into two rooms. This way, no man saw any woman he was not related to in her finery. I looked around and saw that *all* the women were dressed formally, in long, tightly fitted dresses with low necklines. Truly, it looked like a showgirl convention.

I was allowed to peek between the curtains for just a moment. Sure enough, there was a room full of men, much less formally dressed than the women but obviously in high spirits given the laughter and loud conversation.

"Please come and sit here. It is a good table near the dance floor," an unknown lady said. Possibly Miriam had alerted her to my presence since she could speak English.

My attention shifted back to my side of the curtain. Had I heard that correctly—a dance floor? Yes, as the afternoon progressed, the music, from the other side of the curtain where the musicians sat, began to play. Immediately all the women got up and began to dance with one another. *Okay,* I thought, *that's not too strange, given that the men are all secluded.* I was told that they were also dancing with one another. This must have been a real treat for the celebrants as music had been forbidden during the Taliban rule, and it was obvious that the Afghans loved their music.

The women were dancing very provocatively. There was a whole lot of shaking going on. I watched the women closely before being hustled onto the dance floor by my tablemates. As a woman partnered dancing with me, she shimmied up quite close and shook her shoulders and bosom in a suggestive way. I was unsure what was expected of me, so I just mimicked what I saw. Evidently I was a success, as the women pulled back, formed a circle around me, and watched me dance with my partner. I felt uncomfortable, but Miriam called out, "You are doing great dancing, Sue!" She gave me two thumbs up.

Following this very uncharacteristic demonstration from me, women gathered around and started spraying me with something. It looked like shaving cream coming out of a canister. Again, I shot a helpless look at Miriam, who shouted back, "You are wonderful! They love your dancing, so they spray you to honor you."

Dripping from whatever the substance was, I went back to my table, committed to sitting out the next dance. As I watched, I noticed the same scene playing out again and again with various women. Apparently it was the thing to do. I wasn't sure whether the bride was dancing, as I could not pick her out in the crowd, but it seemed everyone was having a good time. The music went on for some time, and when there was a break, the food started to arrive. Lots of delicacies were served—roast lamb, barbecued shish kabobs, rice with raisins and nuts (said to represent fertility), bread, fruits, candies, and fruit juice.

The afternoon sped by, switching back and forth from music, dancing, laughing, eating, and lots of nonalcoholic drinking. The groom never came back to our side of the curtain, I guessed because there were women present that he was not related to.

After a few hours, I was tired and ready to leave. The music was loud, and I thought that I'd stayed long enough not to insult anyone by leaving. I let Miriam and her family know I was leaving. They immediately sent an older woman to the other side of the curtain to get the groom and my colleague, both of whom came to the doorway. The groom was gracious in his goodbye, formally thanking us for attending his wedding. "It has been our honor to have you both here today." Looking at me, he said, "You are the first American woman we have ever met, and you have blessed us by joining us today."

"*Tashakor*," I said, thanking him. "It has been my honor to be included. *Tashakor.*"

As we were leaving, I asked to speak with Miriam again. In all the excitement, I had forgotten to give my gift card to anyone. Someone went to fetch Miriam. I explained about my gift card, and she said she would give it to her sister.

I couldn't help myself and asked, "Did the bride have fun today? She was always looking down and never smiled as she sat on the dais. I don't understand."

"Oh, no, she is very happy to be married, but she must not look too happy or everyone will think she is happy to leave her family," Miriam explained. "But she cannot look too sad either or her new in-laws will think she is unhappy to be joining their family. It is a very delicate balance. Do you understand? Is it not the same with you in America?"

"Our weddings are not exactly like yours," I said. "But this was wonderful and beautiful, and I feel so privileged to have been included in this special family day. Thank you so much."

I returned to the embassy. The machine guns greeted me, and I was enfolded back into a little bit of America on this very foreign soil. As I walked to my camper, a marine came up to me and asked, "What's it like out there in Kabul?"

Oh, it was a riot of color and music today. How could I explain the women, the dresses, the glitter, the dancing, and the loud music? Smiling, I said, "Have you ever been to Las Vegas?"

Chapter 27

Outside Heaven

I was invited by some of our American military advisors to travel with them to the Panjshir Valley north of Kabul. The trip would be a chance for me to see some of the most beautiful countryside in Afghanistan as the Panjshir Valley was famous for its groves of almond trees and fruit trees.

It was a beautiful Saturday morning as I woke up in my little German camper. I was looking forward to the trip and to getting out of my tight quarters for the day.

I fixed a cup of tea in my electric teapot and had a biscuit for breakfast while dressing for the day of travel with my military colleagues. I suspected the military might have a broader agenda than myself for the trip, but that was fine with me. I was going to be a tourist for the day. I wanted to see more of the countryside; I'd heard so many stories of the Panjshir Valley. It was full of the folklore around its most famous son, the now martyred and larger-than-life Massoud, the Lion of Panjshir. The name *Panjshir* literally means "five lions." It was a romantic name for a handsome, noble, and progressive Afghan who had held his ground and saved his villages during two big offenses: once during the Soviet resistance and again during the brutal civil war following the exit of the Soviets. Pictures of Massoud's face were everywhere in Kabul, and I suspected they would be even more plentiful in the valley as he was their celebrated native son. He was reported to be a man who would not compromise his values. It was said that he had been offered key posts in the Taliban government but refused them all on principle. His name carried great weight and was honored among both friend and foe alike for the great warrior he had been. He would be the subject of many songs for generations to come in Afghanistan.

My military escorts arrived right on time. We left the embassy in high spirits for a day of adventure.

As usual, the roads out of Kabul were a congested mess. We inched forward, anxious to hit the open road and make our way north. The day promised to be informative and interesting. Finally the traffic thinned, as did the roadside kiosks as we left town. We passed many people walking along the side of the road going about their morning business. There were very few women in the public spaces, and those we saw were still wearing the blue burqas, even months after the American military and foreign political advisers had arrived.

As we were crossing a bridge on the way north, I was reminded of the day so many months ago when I had traveled to the Salang Tunnel. I was on the same road now and would continue on it for most of the way toward the tunnel before turning east to travel into the Panjshir Valley ninety-four miles north of Kabul.

It was now summer, and even the scarred earth of Afghanistan was coming back to life. I was excited to see the valley in this season after seeing it in the winter when it was an empty white blanket of snow.

As we drove along, we enjoyed the peace of the day and the good weather. The discussion shifted to the charismatic general, Ahmad Shah Massoud, and how he had lived, fought, and died in this beautiful valley. We all wished we had been able to meet him. As expected there was no shortage of posters of him. They were nailed up on posts along the way as well as pasted on the sides of broken buildings and on the old, broken-down Soviet tanks that I had seen from the sky on my last trip north with the ambassador. I felt an attraction for Massoud, who was the local hero and a very handsome man. His charisma was famous among the Afghanis, who spoke of Massoud in an almost mystical fashion. His enigmatic smile looked out at me around each corner. I could see the intelligence and courage in his eyes. He had been dead nine months by this time. We were driving to his home area and would be walking in his footsteps as the day moved forward.

A testament to Massoud's life and the wars he fought was the destruction all around us. There were the many rusted tanks sitting along the roadside like giant, dead toads. Their brown, scarred, and jagged edges bore witness to the years of rotting by the roadside. They were proof that the Soviets had been there, that the Soviets had been beaten, and they had been driven out. While these remnants of war were eyesores and safety risks on the poorly constructed roads, they were also monuments to the courage and tenacity of the Afghan people. The decaying relics of the recent past joined the ranks of the many relics of former empires who had tried to conquer Afghanistan only to be driven out of the forbidding country. They were also monuments of the bravery of villagers, who never gave up. This history was on display everywhere as we drove along.

Once we got further into the countryside, I began to see the graveyards of nut and fruit orchards that had been destroyed by the Soviets in an attempt to starve out and demoralize the Afghan people. It was a canvas of environmental destruction. The hundred-year-old trees could not survive the cruelty of modern-day war.

For centuries, Afghanistan has relied on an ingenious system called *karez* for drinking water and agricultural irrigation. The karez system involves a series of underground canals to move water from the mountains to the valleys. By keeping the water underground, it does not evaporate into the dry air. It is the perfect marriage of nature and technology to serve the needs of the people in the valley.

The system demanded constant maintenance to keep it clean and in good working order. The underground canals had vertical shafts called *chah* that provided workers access across the fields to do underground maintenance. The chahs stick up like little chimneys, dotting the rural landscape where the karez lie below ground. An operational management board made up of elder representatives from each village along the karez service route decided when and how long each branch of the karez would be opened to irrigate the various fields along its miles and miles of construction. It was a complex but fairly operated service of piped-in water.

Many miles of these tunnels and chah shafts had been damaged by war and neglect. Many were willfully destroyed by the Soviets in their effort to subjugate the people. It is often this kind of destruction during war that creates the need for humanitarian assistance because it disrupts the ability of a village to grow its own food or provide clean water for the civilians. Yet, the Afghans entertained no thoughts of giving up, even when their sophisticated networks of karez were destroyed.

As we turned off the main road north to head east, we began to enter the beautiful fields of the Panjshir Valley. Evidence of the destroyed karez system could be seen in the crushed chahs and in the previously fertile fields that were now barren and hungry for water. The hillsides, which rose up sharply on both sides of the long valley, had a purplish-blue hue to them.

As the day progressed, we shared a growing awe for this magnificent country. It must have been physically challenging for the people who lived in these mountains with no modern conveniences to survive even in this rich valley. Still, they loved it so much that they were willing to die rather than to hand over their independence to any outside ruler. I knew that most of the people living in this valley had never seen TV. Surely none of them had known of the World Trade Center and the Pentagon attacks beforehand. The events of 9/11 were why we were all there that day, but we felt strangely removed from those events in the face of the people in Panjshir Valley. They worked hard every day and focused only on their families and friends. They asked for nothing from anyone and yet were willing to offer generous hospitality to any stranger who wandered through their valley. Nothing was asked in return except that the stranger respect their simple ways and leave their valley untouched. It seemed a straightforward enough request in return for their friendship.

I had been in Afghanistan for six months, and I was still surprised at the initial greeting and gracious attitude of the rural Afghans. But I wondered if they were now beginning to ask themselves, "When will these foreigners leave?"

Their valley had been used as a trade route for centuries as caravans moved from east to west and back carrying their treasures. The further away we went from Kabul, the more primitive the lifestyle became. I felt like I was being thrown back hundreds of years in a matter of hours. The valley offered up the simplicity of its ancient lifestyle. The day's activities were dictated by the season, the weather, and the hours of daylight. A man's goal was to eat, survive, and protect his families. Many men had more than one wife and family. Traditions ran strong here, and while hospitality was freely offered, it was expected that the guest would respect their ways. It was hard to be a Western woman, with all my privileges and freedoms, and not judge both the men and the women regarding their gender restrictions and plural marriages. But often, to my surprise, the women seemed content. Maybe it was because they didn't know anything else, but also, in the villages within this valley, the women were respected. Families took care of one another. The reality of these women was far removed from the life of women in Kabul and southern Afghanistan, who had been trapped under the cruel yoke of Taliban laws.

The Panjshir Valley was like the Garden of Eden. Below and between the sharply rising mountains lay this fertile land with the promise of an abundant harvest. The valley and the mountains were in stark contrast to each other. The stony hillsides looked forbidding and inhospitable, while the valleys looked green and fertile. It was July 2002, and the valley held the promise of a fall harvest. I could imagine the wagons full of food, pulled by their strong mountain horses. Kabul was such a sad place, with its bombed-out buildings and slums, when compared to here.

The Panjshir Valley had had its native son to defend it and keep it safe. Kabul had the Taliban.

As in Kabul, the men of Panjshir walked around holding hands, a familiar custom in much of the Islamic world. They wore cream-colored shalwar kameez and brown vests or jackets. Unique to this region, most men wore the brown wool cap of Massoud rather than a turban. The cap was like a beret but with rolled edges and sat straight on the head. It was made of rough, unprocessed wool.

Few women could be seen out in the open. Many practiced *purdah*, the custom of women remaining secluded inside their own compounds that is based on a conservative practice of Islam. There was a slightly different tone, and choice, to practicing purdah than the forced exile of women from the public square in the Taliban-controlled areas. The end results seemed the same to me, but I sensed that the women here took it as their decision to be modest. As a woman, I was occasionally admitted into one of the compounds, but that didn't happen on this outing. We were not meeting with any specific group, nor were we promoting any program.

Our purpose that day was just to be tourists. Also, because I was traveling with the military in uniform and with weapons, I did not expect to be invited into any home or greeted with as many smiles as usual. There was a natural inhibition and reticence on the part of the local population when military personnel walked around.

As noted, the military may have been using the trip to gain strategic knowledge of this region, but for me, it was simply a day in the country. I always kept my eye out for any glaring humanitarian needs, no matter what the reason of any trip. But that day, I was really relaxing for the first time in many months. We stopped in a beautiful spot and had a picnic. Everyone enjoyed themselves even as the military remained vigilant.

As we left the valley, I looked back and thought about the gift of this perfect day for me outside the gates of Heaven. It was all so beautiful and untouched by the outside world.

After the long day of travel, we arrived back at Heaven and were admitted through its gates. I was grateful for what I had seen and grateful to be back home again. It had been a long but restful and peaceful day as I was nearing the end of my assignment in Afghanistan.

Epilogue

It is now 2021, and I look back on nineteen years of change since I was in Afghanistan. The years have been busy for everyone: for my son Jason, for me, and for the Afghans. Life is not what we might have expected back in 2002, but it is mostly good.

Jason has been busy building his life. He took some time to recover from the events of 9/11, working throughout the process. He has become a new man, with some expected and some unexpected changes as result of the trauma of that awful day. He is more thoughtful and has an increased awareness of the tenuousness of life that many do not. He is stronger. He is happy.

As for me, I have piled more wars on top of the Afghan war. I traveled back one more time to Kabul after leaving there in August 2002. I applied for another job there. I was considering an offer to be chief of party for a US government-sponsored program to upgrade the education system and increase the enrollment of girls in school. In the end, I did not take it. It was two years after I had left, but I still did not feel ready to expose myself again to the stress or the trauma of Afghanistan. Instead, I took jobs in a succession of countries that touched me in ways that were new and ways that were the same as in Afghanistan. I worked in Iraq on three assignments, in Yemen on two assignments, and twice in Ukraine. I had a long stint in Central Asia, covering five countries while living in Nepal. And I went back to Africa, a place that I loved but had avoided for some time, to work in Sudan and South Sudan. All in all, I settled on some kind of peace for myself, and I continued to grow in my professional field.

My family is everything to me and have been there consistently, especially my husband, who supports me daily. I know where I belong now. I belong home, and home is in America with family and friends. I will always long for the places and the people I've worked with over the years. I continue to question everything since very little makes sense to me. The poor of the world will always haunt me, as I know their faces and names. The abused are no longer theoretical but are real-life people who suffer daily beyond what the fortunate can realize. I am not sure if I need to dwell in the horrors that occur daily around the world or burden my family and friends with these events, but they are seldom far from my mind or heart. A glass of cold, clean water means so much to me. A safe, sturdy shelter comforts me on cold and rainy nights. I know many who don't have the luxury of warmth. There are times when I think I am a voice of doom and disaster when I pontificate with my patient friends and loyal family, but there are moments when I cannot pull my thoughts away from an article I've just read or a picture I've seen. It is all still very real for me.

I want to share these experiences without burdening others with what they cannot change. I went there—Afghanistan and elsewhere—and I could not change anything. I started my work thinking I would change the world. Then I got more realistic and hoped to change a village. And then reality hit, and I realized that I'd succeeded if I'd help to change one life. Modulating my expectations keeps my frustrations in check most of the time. And every day, I know deep down how very fortunate I am to be where I am and have what I have. All of it is good. I have given myself permission not to have all the answers, to take one day at a time. I'm trying to take the long view of life like my Afghan friends do.

Certainly, I keep up with Afghanistan and weigh the news of current events against the halcyon—yes, even heavenly—days of my time there. In spite of the war, or because of it, when America first went to Afghanistan, there was hope. In those early days the population, especially the women I met, expressed such optimism for their futures. It felt like Afghanistan was on the brink of a new beginning. There have been centuries of armies crossing through Afghanistan with various aspirations. Some may have been noble, but many were not. I thought we were different. I thought we went to give, not take. Al Qaeda drew us there, the Taliban fought us there, and political agendas have kept us there. Now what?

In most ways, the Afghans are so very patient. But about some things they are not. They are patient regarding change but have no patience or tolerance for occupation. After only months in their country, I was being asked, "When will America leave?"

I don't know when the opportune time would have been or will be for us to leave. I read a *Washington Post* article by Ambassador Ryan Crocker, who served with me early in my assignment to Kabul before Ambassador Don Finn arrived. Ambassador Crocker believes that at this time, in this manner of negotiating with the Taliban, we, America, are abandoning many who believed in us. He referred to the dialogue as "negotiating the terms of our surrender" (January 29, 2019, *Washington Post*, "I was an ambassador to Afghanistan. This deal is a surrender," by Ambassador Ryan Crocker). Like him, I am especially worried about the women and girls in Afghanistan who may be pushed back into the horrific, restrictive lives that the Taliban could dictate for them. And there are broader concerns about democracy and governance. Personally, I think these are better left up to the Afghan people to decide, but I hope that whatever they decide will be an inclusive process for all its citizens, not just half of them. The women have much at stake. They were wise back in 2002 to say they would wait to throw off their burqas. They knew nothing was safe then, and the future was unknown. They may have been right. If the Taliban come back into power, men like Ashraf Ghani, who is now president, will likely lose power. He was an odious man to me, but I think that he wants what is best for Afghanistan and is a staunch supporter of women's rights. He and others like him may get negotiated out of power, and then who will take care of the women?

I learned so much about myself, life, and power when I was in Afghanistan. The Afghans are fiercely loyal in their love of family, culture, and country. They can find the heart of a lion in a man and honor him, whether friend or foe. How privileged I was, and am, to have had a chance to see that. Women there are beautiful, smart, and strong. They just need to have the feet of men taken off their necks, as Justice Ruth Bader Ginsberg said when talking about the potential of American women.

The Afghans will never accept occupation. An older gentleman who had good will toward America and who was supportive of America's reason for entering Afghanistan once said to me, "In Afghanistan, the fight is *never over*. What I do not finish this year or in this lifetime, my grandson or his grandson will finish for me." Their view of life is not like ours, but it has served the Afghans well for centuries. They live in generations. The Afghan has not yet begun to count the years of this war.

I walked on ground that I had never in my life imagined I would. I was involved in events, albeit in a very small way, that turned the course of history. The long and proud history of Afghanistan's culture, religion, and people will have to complete that turn.

I expect that Afghanistan will survive, as it has for eons past. I want so much for them. I want their culture of strong, protective men to survive. I want their amazing women to have a chance. I want their beautiful land to be bountiful again, and I want their children to soar. It is my hope that this will come to be for this amazing country and its people.

"Make visible what, without you, might perhaps have never been seen."
Robert Bresson